1001 Sensational Second World War Facts

Scott Addington

1001 Sensational Second World War Facts

1001 Sensational Second World War Facts

Scott Addington

©Scott Addington 2021
All rights reserved.
Cover image: Battlefield Design

1001 Sensational Second World War Facts

Other books by Scott Addington:

1001 Fantastic First World War Facts
WW1: A Layman's Guide
WW2: A Layman's Guide
The Third Reich: A Layman's Guide
D-Day: A Layman's Guide
Waterloo: A Layman's Guide
The Great War 100: The First World War in Infographics
Heroes of WW1
5 Minute History: First World War Battles
5 Minute History: First World War Weapons
Heroes of The Line
Reaching for The Sky – The RAF in 100 Moments
Invasion! D:Day in 100 Moments

All books available from Amazon and other good bookstores world wide.

1001 Sensational Second World War Facts

If you want even more facts, head on over to
www.scottaddington.com
and pick up a free e-book:

500 Fantastic First World War Facts

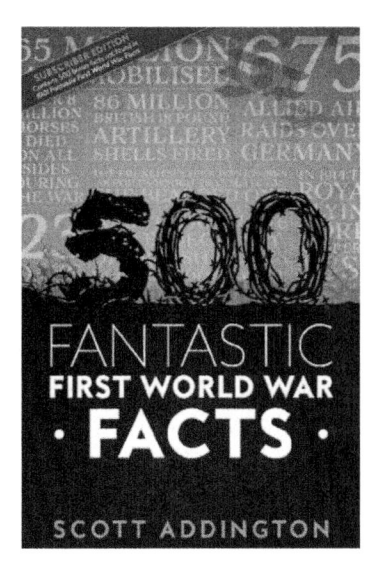

#facttastic

1001 Sensational Second World War Facts

Introduction

Despite the thousands of books written on the Second World War, you can count on one hand how many good, clear, to-the-point fact books have been published over the years. So, after the success of my first fact book - 1001 Fantastic First World War Facts - I decided to right this despicable literary wrong and here we are with 1001 Sensational Second World War Facts.

You're welcome.

To put together a fact book on a subject such as the Second World War is no small undertaking. The sheer vastness of topics to choose from was the first (not inconsiderable) challenge, and don't get me started on how much time it takes to fact check even the most seemingly straight-forward statistic. One thing that this project has taught me is that hardly any of the top-level historians of our day produce data that other historians completely agree with. Perhaps that is down to the sheer difficulty of garnering such statistics in the first place, or perhaps it is simply down to ego. I don't know. What I do know is that I have tried to double/triple check as many facts as possible here to bring you the most factually correct collection of facts in the history of facts. Fact.

Despite my fact-checking heroics, there will, inevitably, be areas where other sources / books / websites / historians etc. will present slight variations and have differing opinions. I have listed out some of my main sources in the *References* section of this book, but these differences are just one of the delights and joys of historical interpretation and are to be expected.

As with my previous fact book, I have continued to use numbers rather than text (for example twelve is written 12) to make the facts easier to read and digest. I have tried to work through the war as chronologically as possible although there are dedicated sections on some of the main combatants and some of the key weapons.

Finally, the focus of this book and the facts within it are purely on the military aspect of the war. As a result, there are very few (if any) facts on the Holocaust or the political side of the NSDAP – I think those subjects deserve and demand fact books of their own. Watch this space...

Finally finally, I must pay tribute to Kris Wiblin, Finn Jacobs, and Matthew Wootten who have cross-referenced, proof read and generally kept both myself and the manuscript on the straight and narrow. Thank you all!

With that, let's get on with the fact-show. I hope you enjoy reading through this collection of facts and statistics from the Second World War and maybe discover a few new things that you did not know before.

SMA 2021

Contents

General facts

Combatants: Britain and the Commonwealth

Combatants: Germany

Combatants: Russia

Combatants: USA

The war in the Air

Weapons

1939

1940

1941

1942

1943

1944

1945

Bravery

Casualties

References

General Facts

1. The Second World War lasted 2,194 days (up until the surrender of Japan)

2. 81 nations were involved in the Second World War

3. The main Allied powers included Britain, The Soviet Union, France, China, India, Australia, New Zealand, South Africa, Canada, and the USA

4. The main Axis powers were Germany, Japan, Italy, Romania, Bulgaria, and Hungary

5. 4 countries swapped sides from Axis to Allied during the war - Italy, Finland, Romania, and Bulgaria

6. Romanian forces fought alongside Germany in the Soviet Union from June 1941, but then switched sides after a coup in August 1944

7. For most of the war Bulgaria was allied with the Axis Powers but in September of 1944 a new Bulgarian government came to power. Bulgaria declared itself neutral, expelled German forces and sought peace with the Allies

8. Finland sided with the Axis Powers to regain territory lost to the Soviet Union in 1939-40 but by August 1944 a new government was in power and quickly started secretly negotiating a peace deal with Russia

9. Italy entered the war in summer 1940 with the aim of picking up British and French territories in Africa but after several military disasters, Mussolini was overthrown and by October 1943 Italy was fighting on the side of the Allies

10. Brazil was the only independent South American country to send ground troops to fight in WW2 - sending 25,000 men

11. During WW2 the Oscar statuettes were made of painted plaster due to a metal shortage

12. The Allies discussed the possibility of dropping glue on German troops to slow their movements

13. The Mosque of Paris helped Jews escape the Nazis by giving them Muslim ID's

14. Japan and Russia still have not signed a peace treaty to end the Second World War due to the Kuril Island dispute

15. Around 22,000 French citizens were honoured by the post-war government for their involvement in the French Resistance

Combatants: Britain & The Commonwealth

16. When Princess Elizabeth (now HRH Queen Elizabeth II) turned 18 in 1944 she insisted on joining the British Army and served as a driver and a mechanic during the war. She remains the only female member of the British Royal Family to have served in the British Army

17. As the war began the UK authorities expected enemy bombing almost immediately and ordered sections of the civilian population to be evacuated from at risk cities. All together 1,471,000 people were evacuated, including 827,000 children

18. Conscription was introduced to Great Britain in April 1939 when single men between 20 and 22 were called up for 6 months' service

19. By the beginning of the war these criteria had been expanded to include all men aged between 18 and 41. In December 1941 the age limit was upped again to 51

20. In September 1939, the British Army numbered 897,000 men. By June 1940 it was 1,656,000

21. 160,000 soldiers of the BEF (British Expeditionary Force) were sent to France in September 1939 - rising to 400,000 over the winter

22. At London zoo all poisonous snakes and insects were destroyed and valuable animals such as a baby elephant and giant pandas were sent to other safer zoos. The zoo remained open throughout the war.

23. The RSPCA put down 400,000 pets in the first weeks of the war in London alone to save food

24. Blackout regulations were in force within days of the war starting. No interior lights were to be visible outside. Offenders could receive a £100 fine and a 3-month prison sentence

25. The blackout offered lots of opportunity for all types of criminals and thieves - crime incidents rose 50% during the war.

26. During the blackout, vehicle headlights had to be masked and street lighting was switched off

27. Between September and December 1939, the number of road accidents doubled from the previous year to 4,133

28. No gas attacks were ever launched on Britain during the war

29. During the war, the number of allotments in Britain almost doubled to 1.4 million

30. There were 1.5million unemployed in Great Britain in 1939. By 1945 that number was just 54,000

31. 214 British Women were jailed for refusing to carry out war work

32. Approximately 6,000 conscientious objectors spent the war carrying out labour and construction jobs

33. Due to food shortages, British scientists considered developing plankton as a human food. Plankton is rich in proteins, fats and vitamin A but it was too difficult to harvest effectively

34. Central London prostitutes were known as Piccadilly Commandos. With the rise in enlisted men living and training in the capital saw a big rise in female sex workers

35. 1,355 Air Raid Precaution (ARP) members were killed during the war

36. Britain was the only country to give its entire population gas masks. 44 million were issued

37. 'Bevin Boys' was the nickname given to the 48,000 men who were conscripted into the coal mining industry rather than the armed forces to prevent a coal shortage. Ernest Bevin was the British Minister for Labour

38. Sir Winston Churchill lost the UK 1945 election, despite winning the war

39. By the end of the war Britain found herself £21 billion in debt

40. Britain finally paid off her WW2 debts on 31 December 2006. The payments of $83.25 million to the USA and $22.7 million to Canada were the last of 50 instalments which the country had been paying since 1950

Combatants: Germany and the Third Reich

41. The German term *Wehrmacht* means defensive power. The three primary branches of the Wehrmacht were the *Heer* (army), *Luftwaffe* (air force), and *Kriegsmarine* (navy)

42. By the end of the war, more than 17,000,000 troops had served in the *Wehrmacht*

43. If Adolf Hitler's father had not changed his surname in 1877, the most famous dictator ever would have been called Adolf Schicklgruber

44. Hitler was prescribed powdered cocaine to clear his sinuses

45. In 1938, Hitler was Time Magazine's 'Man of the Year'

46. During his time in power Hitler's Mein Kampf was given away to all newlywed couples

47. Hitler sentenced 84 of his Generals to death during the war

48. Hans Graf Von Sponek was the first General to be tried and sentenced to death for "failing to obey orders" when he retreated to a much more defensible line at the Battle of Kerch in December 1941. Hitler later commuted the death sentence to time in prison, but Himmler had him executed anyway in 1944

49. Hitler never visited a single concentration camp

50. When Hitler visited Paris, the French cut the lift cables to the Eiffel Tower so if he wanted to climb to the top, he would have had to take the stairs

51. Hitler planned to collect thousands of Jewish artifacts and create a 'museum of an extinct race' after the war

52. Hitler's plan for Moscow was to kill all residents and replace it with an artificial lake

53. The American secret service tried to spike Hitler's food with female hormones to pacify him. They failed

54. The *Führersonderzug* was Adolf Hitler's personal train and served as a mobile headquarters during the early stages of the war when Hitler and his entourage used the train to visit the front line

55. The *Führersonderzug* consisted of between 10 and 16 individual carriages including a dining carriage, sleeping quarters and a communications centre. It also carried its own anti-aircraft guns

56. It was named *Führersonderzug* "Amerika" in 1940, and later in January 1943, the *Führersonderzug* "Brandenburg"

57. In 1945, Hitler's aide and adjutant Julius Schaub saw to it that the *Führersonderzug* was destroyed

58. Germany's power grid was much more vulnerable than realised. One estimate is that if just 1% of the bombs dropped on German industry had instead been dropped on power plants, German industry would have collapsed

59. The SS symbol, seen on flags and the lapels of uniforms, was based on the Germanic sig rune, which means "victory"

60. The SS was divided into 3 primary branches. The *Allgemeine-SS* was the general SS, the *Totenkopfverbände*, or "Death Head Brigade", ran the concentration camps, and the Waffen-SS was a military division that fought alongside German army units, although it had its own leadership structure

61. One of the major differences between the German Army and the *Waffen-SS* was that they were not permitted to surrender on any account. Their sworn allegiance to the Führer was to death

62. The *Waffen-SS* grew from 3 regiments to over 38 divisions during World War II

63. The SS opened a bank account in which they deposited gold, jewels and money taken from Jewish victims. The bank account was under a fictitious name - Max Heiliger

64. Initially membership of the *Waffen-SS* was only open to German nationals who could prove their Aryan ancestry back to 1800, who were unmarried, and without a criminal record

65. These rules were partially relaxed in 1940, and after Operation Barbarossa in June 1941, Nazi propaganda claimed that the war was a "European crusade against Bolshevism" and subsequently formed units made up of foreign volunteers and conscripts

66. By the end of the war over 1,000,000 soldiers in 38 divisions had served in the *Waffen-SS*, including over 200,000 conscripts

67. The *Waffen-SS* had a number of Special Forces similar to the British SOE. They were tasked with special operations such as the rescue of Mussolini, carried out by one of the *Waffen-SS* Mountain Units, the *SS-Gebirgsjäger*

68. In 1943 the 13th *Waffen-SS* Mountain Division of the SS "Handschar" (1st Croatian) became the first non-Germanic *Waffen-SS* division. Composed of Bosnian Muslims, Catholic Croat soldiers with ethnic German officers and non-commissioned officers

69. After the war, the Waffen-SS was named as a criminal organisation at the Nuremberg Trials due to their connection to the SS and NSDAP. As a result, *Waffen-SS* veterans were denied the benefits granted to other German veterans

70. The *Einsatzgruppen*, or "special task forces," were SS deaths squads that followed the advancing *Wehrmacht* on the Eastern Front, killing communist, Jews, and other enemies of the Nazi regime in the process

71. *SS-Obersturmbannführer* Otto Skorzeny was one of the most celebrated and feared commandos of the war. Daring operations such as the rescue of Italian fascist dictator Benito Mussolini and missions behind enemy lines during the Battle of the Bulge made him known as "the most dangerous man in Europe"

72. During the Battle of the Bulge, English-speaking soldiers under Skorzeny's command wore American uniforms and caused chaos behind American lines. US intelligence suggested that Skorzeny himself was leading a raid to kill or capture U.S. General Dwight D. Eisenhower in Paris. This led to Eisenhower plaster 'Wanted!' posters of Skorzeny all over Western Europe

73. Fanta originated in Germany due to difficulties importing Coca-Cola syrup during the war

74. German wartime propaganda suggested that the Third Reich had a highly mechanised and modern army but, in 1939, Germany was one of the least automotive societies in the western world. At the outbreak of war, there were 47 people for every motor vehicle in Germany. In Britain, that figure was 14, in France it was 8, and in the USA it was 4

75. Germany lost 110 Division Commanders in combat

76. By D-Day, 35% of all German soldiers had been wounded at least once

77. The only nation that Germany declared war on was the USA

78. According to a West German report, 3,060,000 German soldiers were taken prisoner by the Soviet Union during the war with more than 1,000,000 of them dying in captivity

79. 22,252 German prisoners chose to remain in Britain after the war had finished

Combatants: The Soviet Union

80. The Red Army was founded in 1918, shortly after the Russian Revolution. It was formed as an army of the working class, and all Russian citizens 18 years or older were eligible to join. Because most of its early members were peasants, the families of soldiers were guaranteed sufficient food rations as well as assistance with farm work during the time their family members were serving

81. The Soviet Lend-Lease agreement with the United States secured supplies of raw materials, armaments, and food, which were vital to maintaining the war machine - preventing mass starvation over the crucial period of late 1942 to early 1943

82. On the outbreak of the war in 1939 the Red Army had an estimated 1,800,000 men in its ranks, of whom 25% were stationed in the Far East

83. By 1941 the Red Army had grown to 3,000,000 men (300 divisions). Most of the men served in unmechanized rifle divisions and were supported by horse-drawn artillery and the cavalry

84. At its peak, an estimated 12,500,000 men and women fought in the Red Army

85. Throughout the war 955,044 women served in the Red Army

86. 80% of Soviet males born in 1923 perished during the war

87. The Red Army strapped explosives to dogs, which were detonated remotely when the animals approached German tanks and armour

88. Joseph Stalin appointed himself Commander-in-Chief of the Red Army on 20 July, 1941

89. A new Soviet Conscription Act was passed on 31 August 1941. The age of military conscription was lowered to 18 for youths without secondary education and 19 for those who had been educated above that level

90. Lyudmila Pavlichenko is a female Red Army sniper who is credited as being among the top military snipers in history as well as the top female sniper of all time

91. Pavlichenko joined the Red Army soon after the Nazi invasion in 1941, dropping out of the University of Kiev where she had been studying history. She soon made her mark on the War with an incredible 309 confirmed kills

92. Acclaimed Ravioli chef Ettore Boiardi (of Chef Boyardee fame) supplied food rations to the Red Army throughout the war. For his efforts he was awarded the Order of Lenin, the Soviet Union's highest decoration

93. In 1942, to dissuade his troops from allowing themselves to be captured, Stalin issued a new policy he called 'Not One Step Backward'. Under this policy, any troops who retreated in face of enemy fire would be gunned down by Red Army "blocking detachments" positioned behind them

1001 Sensational Second World War Facts

94. Janis Pinups was conscripted into the Red Army in August 1944 and while fighting the German army he was wounded and concussed. When he awoke, he was alone and took the opportunity to return home to Latvia. This was an act of desertion which was punishable by death in the Red Army. Once back in Latvia he went into hiding and did not resurface again until 1995 – some 50 years later!

95. During the battle of Stalingrad, the life expectancy of the average Red Army soldier was 24 hours

96. If you were fortunate to be a Red Army officer your life expectancy at Stalingrad was a heady 3 days

97. The Red Army has its own choir that was established in 1928 as the official army choir of the Soviet armed forces. During World War II, the choir travelled from one front to another, making more than 1,500 performances for troops

98. Stalin's son, Yakov Dzhugashvili, served in the Red Army as an artillery officer during the war. He was captured during the German advances into Russia in 1941

99. Presuming that Stalin's own son would be a strong bargaining chip, the Germans offered to swap young Yakov for a captured German Field Marshal. Stalin turned the offer down bluntly, explaining that he would not consider trading a Field Marshal for a lowly Lieutenant

100. Yakov died at the Sachsenhausen concentration camp on 14 April 1943. Captured German archives seem to suggest he was shot while running for the electric fence that surrounded the camp

101. Red Army commander Georgy Zhukov was introduced to Coca-Cola during the war by Eisenhower. Unable to drink the soda back in Russia after the war he arranged for a special batch of clear Coke (known as White Coke) to be made just for him – so it looked like vodka

Combatants: USA

102. The Second World War cost each American citizen $20,388. In contrast, Vietnam cost $2,204

103. The youngest US serviceman was Calvin Graham who enlisted in the US Navy after Pearl Harbor aged just 12 years old. He was wounded in combat and given a Dishonourable Discharge for lying about his age. (His benefits were later restored by an act of Congress)

104. America's defence budget grew from $2 billion in 1940 to an eye watering $60 billion in 1945

105. During the war, 1,700,000 court-martials were held in the USA - representing one third of all criminal cases tried throughout the country

106. 21,000 American soldiers were found guilty of desertion during the war

107. 49 American soldiers were sentenced to the death penalty for desertion, but only 1 soldier - Private Edward Donald Slovik - had his sentence carried out

108. Private Slovik was executed by firing squad at 10:04am on 31 January 1945 near the village of Sainte Marie aux Mines. He was 24 years old

109. Private Slovik was the first American soldier to be court martialed and executed for desertion since the American Civil War

110. The US Army executed 102 of its soldiers during WW2 - all but 1 were for the rape or murder of civilians

111. The US 92nd Infantry Division was the only African American infantry division to see combat in Europe during the Second World War, fighting in Italy from 1944

112. In October 1944, the 761st US Tank Battalion (The Black Panthers) became the first African American Tank unit to see combat in the war

113. The Black Panthers fought in 4 major battles on the Western Front - winning 391 bravery awards along the way

114. When the US Army landed in North Africa, among the equipment brought ashore were 3 complete Coca Cola bottling plants

115. By the end of the war, there were 426,000 USAAF personnel based in the UK

116. Mark Wayne Clarke became the youngest 4-Star General of the US Army when he was promoted on 10 March 1945 aged 48

117. Once the USA had joined the war, American disc jockeys were banned from taking requests from listeners on the radio. It was thought that enemy spies could use the choice of songs as coded messages

118. Almost 1,000,000 US soldiers descended on the UK between 1942 and 1944

119. The basic pay for a British infantryman was £3 15s a month. Unskilled labourers could earn £6 per month

120. US soldiers earned in the region of £12 per month. As a result, they were very popular with young British women!

121. 70,000 British women married American servicemen during the war

122. Approximately 9,000 children were born out of wedlock to American GI fathers

123. By D-Day, Americans forces had shipped over 7,000,000 tonnes of supplies to the United Kingdom

Combatants: Japan

124. One of the reasons the Japanese joined the Axis for WW2 was that they felt let down by the Allies after the end of the First World War. Whereas other Allied nations were awarded large tracts of land after that war, Japan were rewarded with very little

125. The *Kempeitai* was the Japanese equivalent of The *Gestapo*. A secret military police force that arrested and killed anyone suspected of being anti-Japanese

126. During the war, Japan received Jewish refugees, ignoring Nazi protests

127. On 19 October 1944 while planning for the Battle of Leyte Gulf, Japanese Vice Admiral Takijiro Onishi suggested the formation of a special suicide attack unit in a desperate effort to tackle the overwhelming American superiority. Onishi told officers of the 201st Flying Group headquarters: "I don't think there would be any other certain way to carry out the operation than to put a 250 kg bomb on a Zero and let it crash into a U.S. carrier, in order to disable her for a week."

128. Rear Admiral Masafumi Arima was officially credited with the very first *Kamikaze* attack after his damaged plane crashed into the USS Franklin on 15 October 1944. Japanese High Command made a huge fuss of his actions, posthumously promoting him to Vice Admiral

129. The word *Kamikaze* means 'Divine Wind' in Japanese. Kamikaze aircraft were packed with explosives and bombs that the pilot would purposefully crash into enemy shipping to cause as much damage as possible

130. On 25 October 1944, the very first *Kamikaze* Special Attack Force carried out its first mission, attacking the US Navy fleet during the Battle of Leyte Gulf. By the end of 26 October, they had damaged seven aircraft carriers as well as 40 other vessels - sinking 5

131. The peak period of *Kamikaze* attack frequency came during April–June 1945 at the Battle of Okinawa where 1,465 kamikaze attacks took place

132. Towards the end of the war the Japanese used specially built rocket powered attack aircraft for their *Kamikaze* missions. The advantages of these Yokosuka MXY-7 Ohka aircraft where they could reach incredible speeds - up to 600 mph (965 km/h) in a dive, however they had a very short range of flight and had to be carried within striking distance of their targets on the underside of a Japanese bomber - making both aircraft susceptible to attack

133. 852 Yokosuka MXY-7 Ohka aircraft were built. The Allies called these craft Baka Bombs. Baka being Japanese for foolish or idiotic

134. Although the exact number of *Kamikaze* attacks and their results are a cause for much debate, the US Airforce states that approximately 2,800 Kamikaze attackers sank 34 US Navy ships and damaged 368 others, killing 4,900 sailors in the process

135. *Kamikaze* attacks were more successful and accurate than conventional attacks, but it is estimated that only 19% of all *Kamikaze* attacks were successful

136. The Japanese held Allied prisoners in a very dim light. In Japanese culture being taken prisoner was a disgrace and as such they treated enemy prisoners with contempt - they were beaten, starved, overworked, and left to suffer disease and illness with little or no medical help

137. The death rate for non-Soviet Allied prisoners held by the Japanese was 27%. In comparison, the death rate for those prisoners held by Germany was just 4%

138. Around 60,000 members of the Indian National Army fought for the Japanese during the Burma campaign

139. Onoda Hirō was an Imperial Japanese Army intelligence officer who did not surrender at the war's end. Instead, he spent 29 years hiding out in the Philippines until his former commander travelled from Japan to formally relieve him from duty in 1974

140. In Japan, survivors of the atomic bombings are called *hibakusha* - people affected by a bomb

141. On March 24, 2009, the Japanese government officially recognized Tsutomu Yamaguchi (1916–2010) as a double *hibakusha*. Tsutomu Yamaguchi was confirmed to be 3 kilometres from ground zero in Hiroshima on a business trip when the bomb was detonated. He was seriously burnt on his left side and spent the night in Hiroshima. He got back to his home city of Nagasaki on 8 August, a day before the bomb in Nagasaki was dropped, and he was exposed to residual radiation while searching for his relatives. He was the first officially recognised survivor of both bombings

The War in the Air

142. During the war, the Allies dropped 3,400,000 tons of explosives on to enemy targets

143. When Boeing first began manufacturing its so-called Flying Fortress (the B-17) on a large scale, the massive plane featured 9 machine guns and could carry 4,000 pounds of explosives

144. Around 640,000 tons of bombs were dropped on Germany by B-17s during the war

145. The US 8th Air Force shot down 6,098 fighter planes, 1 for every 12,700 shots fired

146. Germany produced 119,907 aircraft of all types, including bomber, transport, reconnaissance, gliders, training, seaplanes and flying boats. Estimates suggest that around 40,000 were completely destroyed with another 36,000 significantly damaged

147. The most produced combat aircraft was the Soviet Ilyushin IL-2 Sturmovik with 36,183 units

148. The Messerschmitt Bf-109 was Germany's most common aircraft with 30,480 built

149. German night fighters were equipped with cannons that could fire directly upwards, allowing them to fire into enemy fuselages from beneath

150. The Soviet Union was the only country to use female aircrew in combat

151. The Soviet 558th Night Bomber Regiment was an all-women unit that attacked German positions in low level raids. The Germans called the pilots 'Night Witches'

152. Between 1942 and 1945 USAAF planes consumed 9.7 billion gallons of fuel

153. An RAF Bomber Command 'tour' comprised of 30 sorties. After completing 2 tours a crew would then be removed from the operational list and would not be forced to fly any more combat missions - although many did volunteer for additional tours

154. There was a 25% chance of a Bomber Command aircrew surviving their first tour of operations. This rate fell to 10% during their second tour

155. Bomber Command suffered 57,205 casualties killed or posted missing - a 46% death rate

156. Possibly the youngest member of Bomber Command to be killed was Flight Sergeant Edward James Wright, Royal Canadian Air Force, who was killed on 30 April 1945 apparently aged just 16

157. On top of the deaths, 8.403 Bomber Command personnel were wounded and another 9,838 became Prisoners of War

158. Bomber Command lost 8,325 aircraft in action

159. Between March 1943 and the early summer of 1944, the life expectancy for bomber crews was very short, with fledgling crews often being lost during their first 12 operations

160. To confuse German air defence systems, RAF bombers would drop tonnes of aluminium strips as they approached enemy territory. These strips were called *Window*

161. RAF airmen were often referred to as *Brylcreem Boys* as they were perceived as being more glamorous than their compatriots in the Army and Navy

162. On average, the German armaments industry lost 9% of output each year during the war due to Allied bombing raids

163. The German *Korfu* detection system was so effective it could identify British bombing radar transmissions while the bombers were still on the ground in the UK

164. A flying ace, fighter ace or air ace is a military aviator credited with shooting down five or more enemy aircraft during aerial combat

165. *Luftwaffe* fighter pilot Erich Hartmann racked up 352 confirmed kills making him the most successful fighter ace in the history of aerial warfare

166. 104 different *Luftwaffe* pilots recorded 100 or more kills throughout the war. Not one Allied pilot reached that milestone

167. The highest scoring non-German ace of the war was Finnish pilot Eino Ilmari "Illu" Juutilainen who was credited with 94 confirmed kills in 437 sorties

168. The highest scoring Allied fighter Ace of the war was Soviet pilot Ivan Nikitovich Kozhedub who was credited with 66 confirmed kills. He was also one of a very select group of pilots to have successfully shot down a Messerschmitt Me 262 jet fighter

169. Kozhedub allegedly shot down two USAAF P-51 Mustang fighters in a friendly fire incident 17 April 1945 after they mistakenly started to attack him

170. The top US Fighter Ace was Major Richard Ira Bong who was credited with shooting down 40 Japanese aircraft

171. South African pilot Marmaduke Thomas St John Pattle, DFC & Bar was the most successful Royal Air Force fighter Ace with 40 confirmed victories

172. The top French fighter Ace was Pierre Henri Clostermann DFC & Bar who achieved 33 confirmed victories while flying with the Free French Air Force and the RAF

173. Messerschmitt Me 163 *Komet* was the world's first rocket powered fighter plane - designed to intercept enemy bombers high over German held territory

174. In July 1944, the Me 163 *Komet* reached 1,130kmh (700mph) on a test flight - an unofficial airspeed record that was unmatched for over a decade

175. The ME 163 *Komet* used a liquid propellant consisting of 2 volatile substances which ignited when mixed. Enough thrust was produced to propel the tiny fighter to an altitude of 39,000 feet in 3.45 minutes. It was the first piloted aircraft to achieve a level speed of 1,000 km/h (621mph)

176. The ME 163 *Komet* made its operational debut on 13 May 1944. Typical dog-fight tactics were to fly vertically through a group of enemy bombers at around 30,000ft, climb up to 35,000 - 40,000 feet before diving back through the same bomber formation. This gave the fighter pilots 2 opportunities to shoot at the enemy

177. ME 163 accidents were common and although 364 machines were built, they only shot down 16 enemy bombers between them

178. The Messerschmitt Me 262 was the world's first operational jet fighter, making its operational debut during the summer of 1944

179. 20,351 Supermarine Spitfires were built in 20 different variations - making it the most widely produced aircraft in RAF history.

180. By 1943 a 14,000 strong workforce (40% of whom were women) were churning out 300 Spitfires a month from British factories

181. Spitfires had a top speed of 371 mph (597 km/h) and a range of 470 miles (760 km)

182. As the war progressed Spitfire performance was continually enhanced and during the winter of 1943 a modified Spitfire clocked 606 mph or Mach 0.89

183. 14,583 Hawker Hurricanes were built - they had a top speed of 340 mph (547 km/h) and a range of around 600 miles (965 km)

184. The Hurricane took on many different roles during the war including night fighting and tank busting - the later resulted in a 40 mm anti-tank cannon being mounted under each wing

185. Churchill agreed to supply Russia with Hurricanes to bolster the Soviet Air Force

186. At the outbreak of war, RAF Bomber Command consisted of just 23 operational squadrons with a total of 280 aircraft

187. During the war, RAF Bomber Command grew rapidly to 126 Squadrons. 32 of these were officially non-British units

188. RAF Bomber Command flew a total of 376,795 sorties during WW2

189. The average age of Bomber Command crew was 21

190. By 1944, 17% of Bomber Command personnel were female

191. It is believed that William Wedgwood Benn DSO DFC, father of Labour politician Tony Benn, was the oldest man to fly operationally; he was born in 1877. He served as a pilot in the Royal Flying Corps in World War I and re-joined as a pilot officer in 1940, rapidly rising to the rank of air commodore; he re-trained as an air gunner and flew operationally several times at the age of 67 until his age was recognised and he was officially "grounded"

192. RAF Coastal command was formed in 1936. Its primary wartime occupation was to protect Allied shipping from enemy attack and protect British ports and coastal areas

193. Coastal Command flew over 1,000,000 hours across 240,000 separate operations

194. Coastal Command destroyed 212 enemy U-boats and 366 German transport vessels

195. During the war over 2,000 gallantry awards were bestowed upon Coastal Command including 4 Victoria Crosses

196. The Avro Lancaster carried a crew of 7: pilot, navigator, bomb aimer, flight engineer, wireless operator, mid gunner, and rear gunner

197. 73,777 Lancasters were built. 3,249 were lost in action

198. The Lancaster's first operational flight took place on 3 March 1942 when 4 Lancasters from No. 44 Squadron carried out some minelaying off the north-west coast of Germany

199. The Avro Lancaster had a range of 2,530 miles (4,072km) and a maximum speed of 287 mph (462 km/h)

200. The maximum bomb load of a Lancaster was either 1 x 22,000lb Grand Slam bomb or 14,000lb (6,350 kg) of smaller bombs

201. Over the course of the war, Lancasters took part in thousands of bombing raids over enemy territory, flying 156,000 individual sorties

202. 10 Lancaster crew members won the Victoria Cross during the war

203. The first British air raid on a concentrated civilian population was over Mannheim on 16 December 1940

204. German Me-264 bombers were technically capable of bombing New York City

205. The Russians destroyed over 500 German aircraft by ramming them in mid-air

206. More US servicemen died in the Air Corps than the Marine Corps. While completing the required 30 missions, your chance of being killed was 71%. Not that bombers were helpless

207. At its peak in 1944, the US Airforce boasted around 80,000 aircraft

208. Project Habakkuk was a plan by the British to build aircraft carriers out of pykrete (a mixture of wood pulp and ice) for use in the Atlantic

The War at Sea

209. In 1939, the Royal Navy was still the largest navy in the world, boasting around 1,400 vessels

210. The Royal Navy's assets were split between 6 main fleets: The Home Fleet, The Mediterranean Fleet, the South Atlantic Station, the American & West Indies Station, the East Indies Station, and the Eastern Fleet

211. There were 200,000 men (including reserves and marines) serving in the Royal Navy at the start of the war, this rose to 939,000 by the end of hostilities

212. At the start of the Second World War the Royal Navy had 15 battleships and battlecruisers with 5 more under construction, along with 7 aircraft carriers

213. At the end of the war the Royal Navy boasted 16 battleships and 52 aircraft carriers

214. During the war, the Royal Navy lost 278 major warships and over 1000 smaller vessels

215. In January 1939 Adolf Hitler ordered 'Plan Z' – the re-armament of the German Navy (*Kriegsmarine*) to a level that would rival the Royal Navy by 1948

216. Germany's main naval weapon was the U-boat; its main mission was to cut off the flow of supplies and munitions reaching Britain by sea. During the war, German shipyards launched 1,162 U-boats

217. German and other Axis submarines sank 2,828 merchant ships totalling 14,700,000 tons

218. German submarines also sank 175 Allied warships, mostly British, with 52,000 Royal Navy sailors killed

219. The first warship sunk in World War II was the destroyer *ORP Wicher* of the Polish Navy by Junkers Ju 87 dive bombers from the German aircraft carrier Graf Zeppelin on 3 September 1939

220. The top U-boat Ace of the war was Otto Kretschmer who sank 47 ships totalling 274,333 tons

221. British Battleship HMS Hood was sunk by the German Battleship *Bismark* on 24 May 1940

222. *HMS Hood* sank in just 3 minutes, of the 1,418 crew on board, just 3 survived

223. The sinking of *HMS Hood* sparked a massive hunt for the *Bismark* which was caught and sunk just a few days later on 27 May with the loss of over 2,000 men

224. The Mediterranean U-boat Campaign lasted from about 21 September 1941 to 19 September 1944

225. Some 60 German U-boats took part in the Mediterranean U-boat campaign to defend Axis supply convoys and to disrupt Allied supply routes

226. The Germans sank 95 Allied merchant ships totalling 449,206 tons and 24 Royal Navy warships including 2 aircraft carriers: *HMS Ark Royal* and *HMS Eagle*

227. German U-Boat losses in the Mediterranean amounted to 62

228. 40,000 men served on U-Boats during World War 2; 30,000 never returned

229. German Submarines (U-boats) would often operate in groups called 'Wolfpacks' where they would form a line across the intended path of their target convoy. Once a convoy approached, they would infiltrate its formation and attack

230. The Germans called the winter of 1940/41 their 'Happy Time' as they were highly successful during this period attacking Allied shipping in the Atlantic

231. As shore-based aircraft could not cover the whole length of convoy routes across the Atlantic there were gaps in the defence where U-boats could attack without risk of air attack - This area was known as the 'Atlantic Gap'

232. The Atlantic Gap was eventually closed with the introduction of long-range aircraft such as Liberators, Sunderlands and B-17's as well as the presence of aircraft carriers along convoy routes

233. The Germans lost 757 U-boats during the Battle for the Atlantic

234. 146 of those U-boats were accounted for by RAF Coastal Command's shore-based aircraft - although this success came at a price as Coastal Command lost 741 aircraft at the same time

235. The Royal Navy used High Frequency Direction Finding (HF/DF) equipment to help locate U-boats by tracing their radio transmissions - known colloquially as *Huff Duff*

236. The Royal Navy also used Asdic submarine detection equipment which was fitted to the underside of ships. It was effective but struggled in rough seas and couldn't detect any U-boats that were on the surface

237. Atlantic casualties were: 25,870 U-boat crewmen; 30,000 Allied Merchant Seamen and 41,000 Allied Royal Navy sailors and RAF airmen

238. May/June/July of 1942 were the most productive 3-month period for the Wolfpacks - who claimed a total of 365 Allied ships sunk in this period

239. In total, 2,828 Allied ships were lost to U-boat Wolfpacks in the Atlantic

240. The fatality rate of German U-boat crews was 63%

241. German U-boat crews dubbed their submarines 'iron coffins'

242. On 27 July 1943, an incident took place near the Aleutian Islands when a US Navy task group began tracking a series of unknown radar contacts thought to be Japanese ships. The order was given to open fire but despite blasting the area with over 500 shells there were no signs of any damaged or sunk vessels in the vicinity. In fact, there were no enemy ships within 200 miles. In an effort to explain away this strange occurrence, US Navy officials suggested their radar had picked up distant mountains, but modern analysis seems to suggest the radar blips could have been migrating birds

243. Allied shipping losses in the Second World War in the North Atlantic, Arctic and Home Waters were just 1.48 per cent

Weapons

244. The deadliest sniper of the war was Finnish sniper Simo Häyhä. Known as 'White Death', he officially killed 505 Soviet troops

245. The United States produced over 1.5 million Thompson submachine guns during the Second World War

246. The M1 Garand was the first self-loading rifle to become standard issue for the United States and allowed US soldiers to fire 8 rounds before needing to reload. General George S. Patton called it 'the greatest battle implement ever devised'

247. The *Maschinengewehr 34* was the quintessential German infantry weapon of the war. It was one of the most reliable and well-built weapons in use, was unmatched in terms of rate of fire (900 rounds per minute) and could be carried by just 1 man

248. Invented by Barnes Wallis, the Grand Slam bomb was 26.5ft long (7.7 m) and weighed 22,000lbs (9,979 kg). It was the heaviest bomb carried during the Second World War

249. A modified Avro Lancaster B.Mk 1 (Special) bomber was designed for the Grand Slam, with a reduced crew of 5, fewer gun turrets and a stronger undercarriage. The Grand Slam was so heavy that in the air, the wing tips of the Lancaster bent upwards by 6–8 in (150–200 mm) until the bomb was released; the aircraft then leapt 200–300 ft

250. After release, the Grand Slam would reach a near-supersonic speed of 1,049 ft/s (320 m/s) and would penetrate deep underground before detonating, damaging the foundations of nearby buildings

251. The Grand Slam was first used on 14 March 1945 when Lancaster bombers from 617 Squadron attacked the Bielefeld viaduct - causing massive damage

252. By the end of the war, 41 Grand Slam bombs had been dropped, mainly against large industrial structures such as bridges, bunkers, and viaducts

253. The German *Karl-Gerät* howitzers were huge self-propelled siege mortars that could fire a 2-tonne shell over a distance of 3 miles

254. There were 6 operational *Karl-Gerät* howitzers built, plus 1 test gun. Each gun had to be accompanied by a rail transporter to move it into position, a crane to load the ammunition and several modified tanks to carry shells

255. The *Karl-Gerät* howitzers were first used in May 1941 during an attack against Soviet defences in Lviv

256. The German railway gun (*Schwerer Gustav*) was the largest calibre rifled weapon ever used in combat (80 cm/31.5 inches) and was the heaviest mobile artillery gun every manufactured weighing 1.3 tonnes

257. The shell fired by *Schwerer Gustav* was the largest and heaviest ever - weighing in at almost 7 tonnes! Yet the gun could fire these huge shells 29 miles

258. The *Schwerer Gustav* was designed to smash through the French defences along the Maginot line, but was not ready in time

259. The *Schwerer Gustav* fired its first massive shell on 5 June 1942 against Soviet positions during the siege of Sebastopol - it had taken 4,000 men 5 weeks to get the gun into position and ready to fire

260. The *Panjandrum* was a strange looking device designed to breach the defences of the Atlantic Wall. Consisting of 2 rocket-propelled wheels, joined by a cylinder filled with explosives. The plan was for it to be launched from a landing craft, accelerate up the beach and blow a hole in the sea wall. Tests throughout 1943 and 1944 were disastrous and it was never used in action

261. The *Krummlauf* was a curved barrel attachment for the German *Sturmgewehr 44* (StG 44) assault rifle, which enabled the weapon to be fired around corners. Conceptually it was a promising idea but in use it was found that the barrel attachment wore out very quickly and bullets tended to shatter on exit

262. The 200 tonne *Panzerkampfwagen 'Maus'* (Mouse), was designed by Ferdinand Porsche in answer to Hitler's desire to have an indestructible super tank. Trials began in 1943 but were beset with problems, especially with the drivetrain and despite being powered by a Daimler-Benz aircraft engine it could only hit a top speed of 12mph. Only 2 prototypes were built

263. In 1939 the Ministry of Supply set up a committee of the principal tank designers from the First World War, with the object of looking into current British tank development. 'The Old Gang', as they were known, came up with a concept for a heavy tank – known as TOG 1 - which was in essence only a slightly modified version of a Great War tank

264. *Cultivator No. 6* was the official name given to a trench digging machine developed by the Royal Navy. Based on an idea that Winston Churchill had had during the First World War he wanted to revive the machine in 1939 when he was First Lord of the Admiralty. The huge 130 ton machine could excavate a trench wide enough for troops to advance behind. It may have worked in the Great War but was utterly useless on the battlefields of the Second World War

265. The *Goliath* was a German miniature tank / tracked vehicle designed to deliver a bomb via remote control. The smaller battery powered version could deliver an explosive package of up to 60 kg. A larger petrol driven version could carry 100 kg of explosives over a range of 650m. 2650 were built but were rarely effective. They were slow and the control wires were often cut

266. The Boulton Paul Defiant entered RAF service in December 1939. It was a turret fighter and as such had 4 .303 machine guns mounted to a powered turret situated behind the pilot. It was designed to attack unescorted bomber formations from underneath, but its lack of forward-facing guns meant it was an easy target for enemy fighters. Although it had some success as a night fighter during the Blitz, it was soon withdrawn from active service

267. The *Windkanone* (Wind Cannon) was a bizarre German anti-aircraft weapon that attempted to knock out enemy aircraft by firing a burst of compressed air in its path. In tests the *Windkanone* worked well, but it failed to achieve any wartime results

268. The V1 stands for *Vergeltungswaffe-1*, German for 'retaliatory weapons' and they were developed to strike back at Britain in retaliation for the bombing of German cities

269. The first V-1 was launched at London on 13 June 1944, just 1 week after D-Day

270. It was powered by a simple pulse jet engine which pulsed 50 times per second which gave it a characteristic buzzing sound causing it to be named "buzz bomb" or "doodlebug" by the British

271. Nearly 10,000 V-1s were launched from sites in Northern France over an 80-day period beginning in June 1944. Targets included London as well as other cities in southern England

272. At the peak of the campaign, more than 100 rockets were hitting Britain a day

273. Each V-1 cost about 5,000 *Reichsmarks* or $2,000 in 1944. The 21-foot-long flying bombs were made mostly from sheet metal and plywood

274. Each V1 took about 350 labour-hours to produce. Slave labourers and concentration camp inmates did most of the work

275. Each V-1 was guided by a rudimentary pendulum gyroscope that kept the machine flying straight and level at a cruising altitude of between 2,000 and 3,000 feet. To aim a V-1, operators simply needed to point the weapon in the approximate direction of the target and set the engine to cut out at the desired distance. Gravity took care of the rest

276. Within days of the initial attack, British air defences were reorganised to meet the new threat. Anti-aircraft batteries were quickly re-positioned along the southern coast of England. By the end of the summer, three-quarters of V-1s launched against Britain were being brought down by flak

277. One of the tactics used by fighter pilots to try and destroy V-1 rockets was to use the airflow over a fighter's wing to raise a wing of the V-1 and force it into a spin. To achieve this, they had to slide the wingtip of their fighter plane to within 6 inches of the lower surface of the V-1's wing which would disturb the airflow over the V-1's wing and cause it to lose control. At least 16 V1s were destroyed this way

278. Of the 10,000 V-1s fired at London, only about 20% reached the city

279. The Allies captured V-1 prototypes in Poland in 1944 and the Russians quickly copied and produced 300 V-1s under the 10Kh nomenclature

280. On 29 March 1945, a V-1 struck Datchworth in Hertfordshire – it was to be the last enemy action of any kind on British soil

281. Eventually, there were 3 V-weapons developed, the V2 was the first ballistic missile, the V3 was a super gun which was never finished

282. The V2 (*Vergeltungswaffe 2* or 'Retribution Weapon 2') was the world's first long range guided ballistic missile

283. The first 2 V-2 rockets were fired on 7 September 1944 and targeted Paris - however both crashed soon after launch

284. The following day (8th) another V-2 was successfully fired at Paris and 2 hit London - killing 3 people

285. The Germans did not formally announce the existence of the V-2 until 8 November 1944

286. The V-2 rocket became the first man-made object to travel into space by crossing the Kármán line during a vertical test flight on 20 June 1944

287. Over 3,100 V-2 rockets were fired at cities such as London, Antwerp, Paris, Maastricht, and Norwich

288. An estimated 2,754 civilians were killed in London by V-2 attacks with another 6,523 injured

289. After the US Army captured the Ludendorff Bridge during the Battle of Remagen on 7 March 1945, the Germans fired 11 V-2 rockets in an effort to destroy the bridge. It was the first time the rockets were used against a specific target and the only time they were fired on a German target during the war

290. On 3 November 1944, the Japanese launched the first *Fu-Go* Balloon bomb - a rubberised silk balloon that carried bombs and incendiary devices from the Japanese island of Honshu, bound for North America

291. Over 9,000 Fu-Go balloons were launched with perhaps 10% reaching America. Only 1 lethal incident was recorded with a pregnant woman and 5 children killed on 5 May 1945 in Southern Oregon after investigating a balloon bomb that had landed in a forest

292. The Japanese developed *Kamikaze* rockets called *Ohka* – or 'Cherry Blossom'. a rocket-power human-guided missile, which was carried by a 'mother' plane and then released towards the target – usually a ship. The pilot would then fire up the rockets and hurtle in at up to 600 mph. Ohka pilots were called *Jinrai Butai* – 'thunder gods' – but only managed to sink 3 Allied ships

293. The Soviet T-34 tank was the most-produced tank of the war with 54,500 units made

294. The most common German tank was the *Panzer IV*. Used throughout the war, around 9000 units were produced in total

295. Introduced in 1942, 1,347 *Tiger I*'s were made. The Tiger's armour was 120 mm thick and boasted a huge 88 mm gun

296. The *Tiger I* had a 6:1 kill ratio - i.e. a typical *Tiger I* destroyed 6 Allied tanks before it was put out of action itself

297. The American Sherman M4 tank was the second most highly produced tank of the war with 49,234 machines made

298. The Siegfried Line was the name given by Allied troops to the mass of German defensive fortifications erected before the war along Germany's western borders

299. To Germans, the Siegfried Line was known as the West Wall

300. The Siegfried Line was begun in 1938 as a short belt of fortifications opposite France's Maginot Line but was later extended to cover 630 km (390 miles)

301. There were over 3,000 observation posts, pillboxes, and bunkers along the Siegfried Line

302. By autumn 1940 the Germans had overrun France and the Siegfried Line was no longer needed. The line was subsequently abandoned, weapons and supplies moved elsewhere, and bunkers and pillboxes locked up

303. With the Allied invasion of France in the summer of 1944 it was clear the old Siegfried Line would be needed to defend Germany. On 24 August 1944, Hitler gave a directive for renewed construction and repair of the old fortifications

304. 20,000 forced labourers and members of the *Reichsarbeitsdienst* (Reich Labour Service), most of whom were 14–16-year-old boys, attempted to re-equip and re-build the line for defence purposes. Local people were also called in to carry out this kind of work, mostly building anti-tank ditches. In total, 360,000 people were involved

305. The first clashes on the Siegfried Line took place in August 1944. At times, as many as 2,000,000 American soldiers were involved in the fighting for the Siegfried Line

306. The first atomic weapons were built by the Manhattan Project, a top-secret effort authorised by President D. Franklin Roosevelt in late 1942

307. The assembly line for the atomic bombs was spread out over a great distance. Fuel was manufactured at 2 major sites: The Uranium for "Little Boy," was made in Oak Ridge, Tennessee, whereas the plutonium for "Fat Man," was created at the Hanford Engineer Works in Washington State. The most sensitive work was conducted at a third major site: the laboratory in Los Alamos, New Mexico, close to the Trinity test site in the desert

1939

308. On 23 August, Germany and the Soviet Union sign a non-aggression pact

309. On 31 August, Germany announced that Polish troops had attacked a German radio station near the border and were shot by German soldiers

310. That initial Polish attack was a lie. SS soldiers had dressed up concentration camp prisoners in Polish army uniform and shot them to make it look like an attack

311. On 1 September 1939 Germany retaliated and attacked Poland with 52 German army divisions

312. The Invasion of Poland saw the use of *Blitzkrieg* tactics for the first time

313. *Blitzkrieg* means 'Lightning War' and combined aircraft, tanks, artillery, and infantry assaults that were designed to knock out the enemy before they had a chance to react

314. On 3 September at 11.15am British Prime Minister Neville Chamberlain addressed the nation via radio to tell the country they were now 'at war with Germany'

315. The period between September 1939 and May 1940 was known as 'The Phoney War' in the USA and Britain and the *Sitzkrieg* (The sitting war) in Germany

316. On 17 September, the Soviet Union commenced an invasion of Poland from the east. Warsaw surrendered a week later, and the 2 nations shared their newly acquired prize

317. Germany acquired 73,000 square miles of Poland. Russia took 77,000 square miles

318. Around 694,000 Polish troops were taken prisoner by German forces in the attack. Another 200,000 were killed or wounded

319. Around 16,000 members of the Polish elite, such as priests, aristocrats, university staff and Jews were rounded up and murdered by mobile killing groups called *Einsatzgruppen*

320. German losses during the invasion of Poland were circa 44,000

321. The advancing German troops destroyed 531 Polish villages during the attack

322. 28 October 1939 saw the first German aircraft to be shot down on UK mainland

323. On 30 November 1939, the Soviet Union launches an attack on Finland in what becomes known as 'The Winter War'

324. For the Finland attack the Red Army had 465,000 men against just 130,000 Finns

325. During the Russian invasion, Finnish troops attacked Soviet tanks with homemade bombs. Bottles filled with petrol had flaming rags stuffed into their necks and proved to be highly effective against enemy tanks. They became known as the 'Molotov Cocktail'

326. On 18 December 1939, 12 Wellington bombers were shot down during a daylight raid on enemy shipping near Heligoland. Another 3 were so badly damaged they had to be written off and another 3 crashed on landing. Daylight raids were subsequently abandoned

1940

327. On 9 April 1940, Germany commenced the invasion of Denmark and Norway- effectively ending the 'phoney war'

328. The Denmark/Norway campaign was designed to give Germany control of the North Sea waterways. The code name given for the mission was Operation *Weserübung* (Water exercise)

329. Although the Danish Army was warned of the impending attack, it was denied permission to deploy or prepare defensive positions as the Danish government did not want to give the Germans any provocation for their actions. Only small and scattered units of the frontier guard and elements of the Jutland division were available to meet the land invasion.

330. King Christian X of Denmark thought his army didn't stand much of a chance against the Germans and to save lives he ordered the Danish surrender within 6 hours

Case Yellow

331. On 10 January 1940 Major Helmuth Reinberger was travelling to Cologne by air when his plane crash landed near the Belgian town of Mechelen. Reinberger was carrying plans pertaining to 'Case Yellow' – the proposed German invasion of Belgium, The Netherlands, France and Luxembourg. Despite trying to destroy the files after the crash both he and the documents were captured by Belgian authorities. At that time 'Case Yellow' was scheduled for 17 January

332. Not surprisingly, when Hitler found out about the Mechelen incident he was furious. On 12 January, General Alfred Jodl, the Wehrmacht Chief of Operations wrote in his diary 'If the enemy is in possession of all the files, situation catastrophic!' Eventually, due to this situation and bad weather, Hitler agrees to postpone Case Yellow

333. On 10 May 1940 Germany launches the delayed 'Case Yellow' (*Fall Gelb*) and begins the invasion of Belgium, The Netherlands, France, and Luxembourg

334. On the same day, 10 May 1940, Winston Churchill becomes Prime Minister of Britain

335. For Case Yellow Germany called upon 135 Divisions and 2,700,00 men. The combined Allied defence totalled 151 Divisions and 3,700,000 men

336. On 10 May 1940, when the Germans attacked France, only 16 of their 135 divisions were mechanised – that is, equipped with motorised transport. The rest depended on horse and cart or feet. France had 117 mechanised divisions

337. The Maginot Line was a complex line of bunkers and fortifications built along France's border with Switzerland, Germany, and Luxembourg. Built between 1929 and 1939 it was the French response to German re-armament

338. There were 500,000 French soldiers stationed along the Maginot Line. However, when Hitler invaded Belgium he attacked through the undefended Ardennes forest - thus outflanking the Maginot Line

339. Just 5 days after the initial invasion of The Netherlands, the Dutch army surrenders to Germany on 15 May 1940

340. France also had more guns: Germany had 7,378 artillery pieces and France 10,700

341. On the first day of the attack German aircraft attacked 50 French airfields

342. In just 10 days the German army advanced 200 miles during Case Yellow

343. By the summer of 1940 it is estimated that there were around 8,000,000 Belgian, Dutch and French civilian refugees

344. Axis troops deployed in the Battle of France amounted to about 3,350,000

345. *Blitzkrieg* required men to fight hard and long. In 1940 German military leaders approved sending 35,000,000 tablets of Pervitin and Isophane to the front line to be distributed to the troops. These methamphetamines were used to enhance the stamina of the men - they were able to stay awake for days and work harder and longer without fatigue

346. Italy declared war on Britain and France on 10 June 1940

347. Italy's first offensive was launched through the Alps without German knowledge and ended with 6,000 casualties, with over a third being attributed to frostbite. French casualties were just 200

348. France surrendered to German forces on 22 June 1940

349. Approximately 20,000 French women were forced to have their head shaved for alleged collaboration with German servicemen

Dunkirk & the Fall of France

350. By 21 May the Advancing German offensive had trapped the BEF, 3 French field armies and Belgian forces along the northern coast of France

351. The British started planning the evacuation of the BEF on 20 May - without informing the French

352. Late on 23 May, the German army was told to halt its advance on the trapped Allied forces - Due to a worry that the marshy ground around Dunkirk would be unsuitable for advancing tanks, the decision had been taken to let the Luftwaffe destroy the trapped Allied forces from the air

353. The evacuation of Dunkirk was code-named *Operation Dynamo*. This plan took its name from the dynamo room (which provided electricity) in the naval headquarters below Dover Castle, where Vice Admiral Bertram Ramsay had planned the operation

354. In the beginning the British thought they would be lucky to rescue 50,000 men from Dunkirk

355. In total 338,226 troops were evacuated from Dunkirk between 27 May and 4 June 1940

356. 98,780 men were lifted from the beaches: 239,446 from the harbour and mole (a wooden breakwater protecting the harbour) at Dunkirk

357. 47,081 men embarked from the mole during the devastating *Luftwaffe* air raid of 1 June

358. 933 ships took part in *Operation Dynamo*, of which 236 were lost and 61 put out of action

359. Because of the shallow waters at Dunkirk, British destroyers were unable to approach the beaches, and soldiers were having to wade out to sea to await rescue, many of them waiting hours shoulder deep in water

360. To improve this situation on 27 May the British Ministry of Shipping contacted boat builders around the coast, asking them to collect all boats with a "shallow draft" that could navigate the shallow waters

361. Hundreds of 'little ships' were either taken without their owners' permission or volunteered up willingly. Pleasure boats, fishing vessels, motorboats, yachts and lifeboats were all taken

362. When they reached France, some of the boats acted as shuttles between the beaches and the destroyers, ferrying soldiers to the larger warships. Others carried hundreds of soldiers directly back to England, protected by the RAF. Then turned around and went back for more

363. The number of 'little ships' that sailed on their own initiative will never be known but it is estimated that around 700 took part

364. French, Belgian, Dutch and Norwegian ships took part in the operation alongside the ships of the Royal Navy

365. The BEF left the following equipment behind in France, much of it to be recycled by the German Army - 2,472 guns, 63,879 vehicles, 20,548 motorcycles, 76,097 tons of ammunition, 416,940 tons of stores

366. The shortage of army vehicles after Dunkirk was so severe that the Royal Army Service Corps (RASC) was forced to raid scrap yards for obsolete bus and coach models and use them as troop transports

367. 68,719 men of the BEF were captured wounded or killed during *Blitzkrieg*, retreat and evacuation

368. 40,000 French troops were taken into captivity when Dunkirk fell

369. 177 RAF aircraft was lost during the evacuations of Dunkirk

370. 126 merchant seamen died during the evacuation

371. Churchill had been Prime Minister for only 16 days when the evacuation began

372. The threat of invasion was so real that on 29 May Churchill proposed laying gas along the beaches of the south coast

373. 1,000 Dunkirk citizens died during air raids on 27 May

374. The last of the British Army left on 3 June, and at 10:50, Captain William Tennant - in charge of the evacuation on the ground - signalled back to Vice Admiral Ramsay to say "Operation completed. Returning to Dover." However, Churchill insisted on going back for the French, so the Royal Navy returned on 4 June in an attempt to rescue as many as possible of the French rear-guard. Over 26,000 French soldiers were evacuated on that last day

375. The success of the Spitfire over Dunkirk came as a surprise to many in the *Luftwaffe* who were convinced that their Messerschmitt Bf 109E was the superior fighter of the war

376. The Spitfire and the Bf 109E were very closely matched and in combat a victory was almost always down to tactics and who had seen who first

377. The Dean of St. Paul's referred to the evacuation as a "miracle" - a term that Churchill used many times in public along with references to the "Dunkirk spirit" - the triumph in the face of adversity - which is still lauded in Britain today

378. The port of Dunkirk was captured by the German Army on 4 June 1940

379. *RMS Lancastria* was a British ocean liner requisitioned by the UK Government during the war. She was sunk on 17 June 1940 whilst bringing back British nationals and troops who were still stranded in France. Estimates suggest between 3000 and 5800 people died

380. The sinking of the *RMS Lancastria* remains to this day Britain's worst maritime disaster in history - greater than the Titanic and Lusitania combined

381. Following the sinking of the *Lancastria*, Prime Minister Winston Churchill imposed a media blackout. Eventually, newspapers in New York broke the story at the end of July - five weeks after the disaster. Even then, the British newspapers toed the patriotic line

382. On 14 June 1940 the first German troops entered Paris

383. On 17 June, French Commander Philippe Petain asked the Germans for an armistice to end the Battle of France

384. The Battle of France lasted just 46 Days

385. Approximately 53,000 French civilians were killed by bombing

The British Home Front

386. The project to evacuate British civilians at the beginning of the war was called Operation Pied Piper - it officially began on 1 September 1939

387. In the first 3 days of official evacuation, 1.5 million people were moved: 827,000 children of school age; 524,000 mothers and young children (under 5); 13,000 pregnant women; 70,000 disabled people and over 103,000 teachers and other 'helpers'

388. During the evacuations, the Bank of England moved to the small town of Overton, Hampshire and in 1939–40 moved 2,154 tons of gold to the vaults of the Bank of Canada in Ottawa

389. The Children's Overseas Reception Board (CORB) approved 24,000 children for evacuation overseas. Between June and September 1940, 1,532 children were evacuated to Canada, 577 to Australia, 353 to South Africa, and 202 to New Zealand

390. The CORB scheme was cancelled after the City of Benares was torpedoed on 17 September 1940, killing 77 of the 90 CORB children aboard

391. Almost 300,000 people were charged with Blackout offences in 1940

392. When the Café de Paris restaurant and nightclub in Piccadilly suffered a direct hit by the Luftwaffe in 1941, rescuers had to battle their way through looters that were fighting to tear rings and other jewellery from the dead revellers

393. Clothing rationing commenced in Britain in June 1940

394. By the end of the war 59,192 conscientious objectors had been registered in Britain

The Battle of Britain

395. The Battle of Britain was an aerial battle between the Royal Air Force and the *Luftwaffe*. It started on July 10, 1940

396. The Battle of Britain has an unusual distinction in that it gained its name prior to being fought. The name is derived from a famous speech delivered Winston Churchill more than 3 weeks prior to the generally accepted date for the start of the battle

397. On 13 August 1940 (*Adlertag* or Eagle Day) the Luftwaffe launched 1,485 sorties during 10 hours of raids focussed on RAF bases the South of England

398. The RAF retaliated on Eagle Day with 727 separate sorties of their own to intercept and take down the German bombers

399. RAF Fighter Command claimed to have shot down 78 enemy aircraft during *Adlertag* - Actual German losses were 47 or 48 aircraft destroyed with another 39 damaged

400. The *Luftwaffe* claimed to have destroyed 88 RAF planes in the air and another 84 on the ground. Actual RAF losses that day were 24 aircraft in the air and another 47 destroyed on the ground

401. The Hurricane had a 're-arm and re-fuel' time of just 9 minutes. Compared to 26 minutes for the Spitfire

402. Coastal shipping convoys and shipping centres, such as Portsmouth were the main targets initially. During August, the *Luftwaffe* shifted its attacks to RAF airfields and infrastructure in an effort to destroy Fighter Command

403. The main reason the Germans launched the Battle of Britain was to gain air superiority over Britain in preparation for a seaborne invasion of the south coast

404. The planned Nazi invasion of Great Britain was codenamed *Unternehmen Seelöwe* (Operation Sea Lion)

405. The main RAF fighter planes were the Hawker Hurricane and the Supermarine Spitfire. The German Luftwaffe fighters were the Messerschmitt Bf110 and Messerschmitt Bf109E

406. The Bf109E was also used as a jagdbomber (fighter bomber) and modified planes could carry a 250 kg bomb underneath the fuselage. Unlike the Stuka, the Bf 109, could resume as a fighter after releasing its bomb

407. Hurricanes outnumbered Spitfires in RAF Fighter Command by about 2:1 when war broke out

408. The *Luftwaffe* had more planes than the RAF and their pilots were more experienced

409. It is estimated that around 1,000 British planes were shot down during the battle, while over 1,800 German planes were destroyed

410. The German Junkers Ju87 bomber was better known as the 'Stuka' - taken from *Sturzkampfflugzeug*, the German word for dive bomber

411. By summer 1940, there were about 9,000 pilots in the RAF for approximately 5,000 aircraft, most of which were bombers

412. Only about 30% of the 9,000 pilots were assigned to operational squadrons - the rest were training other pilots, gaining extra qualifications themselves or working in staff and administrative roles (RAF policy dictated that only qualified pilots could make strategic operational decisions)

413. A small element of the Italian Air Force took part in the latter stages of the Battle of Britain on the side of the Axis

414. For Fighter Command, ensuring there were enough trained pilots to fly their planes was their single biggest issue of the battle

415. 18 August 1940 was dubbed 'The Hardest Day' as it was the day that both sides lost the largest number of casualties in a single day

416. During 'The Hardest Day' the *Luftwaffe* flew 970 sorties over Britain. RAF Fighter Command flew 927 sorties

417. 2,936 pilots flew at least 1 operational sortie with the R.A.F. during the Battle of Britain between 10 July and 31 October 1940

418. 595 of these pilots were non-British

419. During the Battle of Britain 1,495 aircrew were killed. 449 were fighter pilots, 718 aircrew were from Bomber Command, and 280 were from Coastal Command

420. The names of these fallen airmen are inscribed in a memorial book which rests in the Battle of Britain Chapel within Westminster Abbey

421. At the height of the Battle of Britain, the need for pilots was so great some were thrown into action after just 10 hours flying experience

422. The average age of an RAF fighter pilot was just 20

The Blitz

423. Central London is bombed by the *Luftwaffe* for the first time on the night of 24/25 August 1940

424. In retaliation, just 24 hours later the RAF bombed Berlin during the night of 25/26 August

425. On 7 September, Germany shifted its focus away from RAF targets and towards London, and, later, other cities and towns and industrial targets also. This was the start of the bombing campaign that became known as the Blitz

426. The first bombing raid of the war actually came on October 16, 1939 when the *Luftwaffe* targeted ships in the Firth of Forth in Scotland

427. At about 4pm on 7 September 350 German bombers, accompanied by 650 fighters flew up the Thames estuary and attacked the docks of east London. A second wave appeared over the city at around 8pm. 448 Londoners were killed that day with another 1600 injured

428. London was bombed for 57 consecutive nights from 7 September 1940

429. British Prime Minister Winston Churchill and his cabinet used Down Street tube station as their bomb shelter, to keep themselves safe from the onslaught of the Blitz

430. At this time, as many as 180,000 people per night sheltered within the London underground system

431. Liverpool and the wider Merseyside area was the most heavily bombed region of Britain outside of London

432. On 14 November 1940, 515 bombers from *Luftflotte 3* dropped over 500 tonnes of high explosives and over 36,000 incendiary bombs onto the city of Coventry

433. At one point during the Coventry raid, 200 separate fires were burning

434. More than 41,000 houses were damaged in the Coventry raid, with 2,306 destroyed. Almost one third of the city's housing was left inhabitable

435. Delighted with the destruction the *Luftwaffe* had caused to Coventry in a single raid, the German propaganda ministry invented a new word – *Coventrieren* or to 'Coventrate' - which meant to devastate via heavy bombing

436. The 200-bomber raid on Belfast on 15 April resulted in the deaths of some 900 residents, making it the deadliest single night attack upon any UK city outside of London

437. The rubble from bombed cities was used to lay runways for the RAF across the south and east of England

438. The Blitz claimed approximately 40,000 lives with another 40,000 injured. Around 1,400,000 people were made homeless

439. *Operation Sea Lion* was postponed indefinitely by Adolf Hitler on 17 September 1940. In the end it was never carried out

440. Italian forces moved into the Western Desert from the Italian colony of Cyrenaica (a region of modern-day Libya) in September 1940. Despite huge numerical superiority over the small British garrison in Egypt they were soon surrounded and on the brink of total defeat

441. Britain attacks Italian fleet at Taranto on 11 November 1940

Operazione E & Operation Compass

442. On 13 September 1940, the Italian 10th Army advanced into Egypt in *Operazione E*, advancing almost 60 miles (95km) in just 3 days, before digging in at Makita to await reinforcements

443. In response to the Italian advance, the British Western Desert Force planned a short, 5-day raid on the Italians to check their progress

444. The raid was called *Operation Compass* and was the first large scale British led military operation of the African campaign

445. The Western Desert Force (WDF)consisted of around 36,000 men. They advanced on the Italian positions on 9 December. The Italians had around 150,000 men

446. The WDF quickly defeated the Italians in their fortified defensive posts and, pushing home their advantage, eventually pushed the Italian 10th Army out of Egypt taking Tobruk (21-22 January 1942), Benghazi (7 February 1942) and El Agheila (9 February 1942)

447. Over 138,000 Italian prisoners were captured, along with hundreds of tanks and thousands of artillery pieces. WDF losses were 1,900 men killed or wounded

1941

Africa & the Siege of Tobruk

448. In February 1941, Hitler sent Erwin Rommel to Africa to bail out the floundering Italians. He immediately went on the attack and succeeding in pushing all Allied troops out of Libya with the exception of Tobruk

449. In his first 2 months in Africa, Rommel transformed the Axis forces located there and advanced 450 miles. The only place that held out any resistance to his *Afrika Korps* was Tobruk

450. Rommel wore British tank goggles on top of his cap as a trophy following the capture of Mechili on 8 April 1941

451. For 241 days, the garrison at Tobruk held firm against constant German assaults. During the winter of 1941 Tobruk was successfully relieved during *Operation Crusader* and Rommel was forced to withdraw and re-organise

452. The Allies broke out from Tobruk in November 1941 with a huge superiority in tanks (600 against 249 *Panzers*) and aircraft (550 vs just 76 *Luftwaffe* machines)

453. *PanzerArmee Afrika* attacked Tobruk again on 20 June 1942 with massed air support - the city fell the next day

454. The Germans took 33,000 prisoners during the capture of Tobruk - it was the second largest defeat of the war for the British after the Battle of Singapore

455. After the fall of Tobruk, the Germans changed tactics - their planned invasion of Malta was postponed in favour of an all-out assault on Egypt instead

German invasions of Yugoslavia, Greece, and Crete

456. On 6 April 1941 Axis forces invade Yugoslavia and Greece

457. Hitler signed Directive 28 authorising *Operation Merkur* (Mercury) for the invasion of Crete on 25 April. The British were first made aware of the plans to invade Crete on 26 April after they intercepted and decoded a *Luftwaffe* message

458. On 20 May Germany begins its planned invasion of the Greek island of Crete during *Operation Merkur*

459. To invade Crete, Germany used 22,000 *Fallschirmjäger* (paratroopers) and men from the 5th Mountain Division in what was the first airborne invasion in military history

460. The German plan hinged on quickly capturing the airfields of Maleme, Rethymno and Heraklion so that reinforcements could be flown in by air

461. German military intelligence organisation, the *Abwehr*, thought there would be only 5,000 British troops on Crete and no Greek forces. In reality, there were over 40,000 British, Dominion and Greek defenders on the island

462. The *Abwehr* also thought that the Cretans would welcome the Germans as liberators. This was not the case with the locals being the first civilian population to offer any serious resistance to the German war machine

463. At the end of the first day of the battle for Crete, the German invaders had not been able to secure any of their objectives

464. Despite having been able to intercept German intelligence messages, the Allied commanders in Crete thought the main attack would come from the sea. Instead of committing all of their resources into an immediate counter-attack, they gave the order to withdraw further inland, allowing the Germans to consolidate their positions

465. On 26 May, as the German advance stalled, they called in for help from the Italians who landed 3,000 men on the south side of the island on 28 May

466. The order to evacuate the island was given on 26 May. From 28 May - 1 June almost 19,000 men were evacuated to Egypt with the help of the Royal Navy

467. Italian and German forces linked up during the night of the 30 May. On 1 June the remaining defenders of the island formally surrendered

468. Crete was a humiliating defeat for the British. Almost 4,000 men were killed and over 12,000 more captured

469. Despite the surrender, about 500 Commonwealth troops remained scattered throughout the island. Working together with local partisans, they continued to disrupt and harass the German occupation long after the official withdrawal

Operation Barbarossa

470. *Operation Barbarossa* was born with *Führer Directive 21*. Signed on 18 December 1940, it set out the intention to "crush Soviet Russia in one rapid campaign"

471.   *Operation Barbarossa* was part of the larger German *Generalplan Ost* which aimed to use the Russians as slave labour for the Axis war effort while acquiring vast agricultural resources and the oil reserves of the Caucasus to help feed and fuel the Reich

472.   *Operation Barbarossa* was named after Frederick I who was crowned King of Germany in 1152 and proclaimed as the Holy Roman Emperor in 1155 until his death in 1190. He was known as Frederick Barbarossa due to his remarkable red beard

473.   In February 1941, British and American intelligence learned of the planned invasion of the USSR. Hoping to encourage Stalin to act against Hitler, they informed him of the plan. Stalin did not believe them, as he believed that Hitler would stick to their pre-war non-aggression pact

474.   In Hitler's original plan the invasion of Russia was set to begin on May 15. However, because of logistical problems and because they had to provide support to Italian forces in the Mediterranean and Africa those plans had to be postponed

475.   At around 03:15 on 22 June 1941, the Axis Powers commenced the invasion of the Soviet Union. More than 3,000,000 men attacked along the 3,000 km (1,865 miles) front, making it the largest military invasion in human history

476.   On the first day of the invasion, the *Luftwaffe* started a strategic bombing of Soviet air and naval bases. They succeeded in destroying around one quarter of the Soviet air force

477. The Germans invasion spanned a front that ran from the Baltic to the Black Sea, a distance of some 1,900 miles (3,060 km)

478. They were divided into 3 army groups – Army Group South under Field Marshal Gerd von Rundstedt, Army Group North under Field Marshal Wilhelm von Leeb, and Army Group Centre under Field Marshal Fedor von Bock

479. The initial invasion force included 3,350 tanks, 7,146 artillery pieces, and 1,950 aircraft

480. Transport was provided by 625,000 horses and 600,000 motor vehicles

481. The news of the invasion was broadcast via radio to the German public during the morning of 22nd June by Propaganda Minister Joseph Goebbels

482. The attack opened the Eastern Front. In Russia it is called the Great Patriotic War

483. It is often thought that the Soviets held huge numerical advantages on the Eastern Front, but this was not always the case, especially at the beginning. On 22 June 1941, the 4 Soviet western military districts between the Baltic Sea and the Black Sea had 2,300,000 men, opposed to nearly 4,500,000 Axis troops. (3,500,000 from the Wehrmacht, 600,000 Romanians and 530,000 from Finland

484. The Finnish army supplied 17 divisions and 2 brigades. Following the Soviet invasion of Finland earlier in the war, they were eager for revenge

485. By 11 July 1941, the Germans had taken more than 400,000 prisoners of war on the Eastern Front

1001 Sensational Second World War Facts

486. By the end of July, just over a month into the invasion, they had seized a chunk of the Soviet Union over twice the size of France

487. In the Baltic states and parts of Belorussia and Ukraine, the Germans were welcomed as liberators throwing out the Russian Communist oppressors

488. To keep the war effort going, Stalin had entire factories moved eastwards so that they could keep on manufacturing aircraft, tanks, and other equipment

489. When foreign diplomats were evacuated from Moscow in preparation for a siege, the embalmed body of former Soviet leader Lenin went with them. His loss was considered too terrible a propaganda blow for the Soviets to risk leaving him there

490. When the Red Army counter-attacked at Moscow in December 1941, the Soviets were able to muster 576,500 soldiers and 574 tanks against German Army Group Centre – which at the time had between 1,200,000 and 1,900,000 troops with 1,800 tanks and assault guns

491. As German troops moved deeper into the Soviet Union, supply lines became longer. Stalin gave instructions to the retreating Red Army to destroy anything that could be of use to the enemy. Soviet soldiers polluted wells, destroyed farm buildings, and poured petrol over any food stocks that could not be moved

492. It is estimated that during the first year of invasion, over 1,000,000 communists were executed by the SS

493. The siege of Leningrad began on 8 September 1941 and was a long-term military blockade aimed at forcing the city (now St Petersburg) to surrender

494. In 1939 Leningrad was responsible for 11% of all Soviet industrial output and as such was one of the main strategic targets for Operation Barbarossa

495. It is estimated that up to 1,500,000 soldiers and civilians died during the siege of Leningrad with another 1,400,000 (mainly women and children) evacuated away from the city - ensuring the siege of Leningrad is ranked as the most lethal siege in history

496. Although Soviet forces managed to force open a small land corridor into the city on 18 January 1943, the blockade remained in place for 872 days - making it one of the longest sieges in history

497. During the winter of 1941/42 the civilians of Leningrad were forced to survive on 125 grams of bread a day - bread that was made up of 50% sawdust. Such levels of starvation plus winter temperatures dropping to -30C (-22F) saw 100,000 deaths a month at its peak

498. On 26 September 1941 Operation Typhoon - the German offensive for the capture of Moscow - was launched in perfect weather conditions

499. In Moscow over 100,000 men were mobilised as militia and 250,000 civilians (mostly women) began to dig anti-tank ditches

500. On 9 October 1941, a day after the key city of Orel fell into German hands, Otto Dietrich told press correspondents in Berlin that 'For all military purposes Soviet Russia is done with. The British dream of a two front war is dead'

501. On 19 October, Stalin declares a state of siege in Moscow

502. By 15 November, after initial success, the German advance on Moscow is paralysed due to freezing temperatures and the ever-increasing Russian defensive force

503. By 27 November 1941, some German panzer forces reached the Volga canal, a mere 19 miles from the northern outskirts of Moscow but were stopped by fanatical Soviet counter-attacks

504. On 5 December Hitler begrudgingly agrees to abandon the Moscow offensive for the winter, German troops begin to withdraw to safer defensive positions

505. A British government report in August 1941 found that just 20% of RAF bombers managed to get within 5 miles of its target

506. On 19 August the first attempt to storm Stalingrad is attempted by German forces

507. The Battle of Stalingrad begins on 23 August

508. On 30 September, during a speech in the *Berlin Sportpalast*, Hitler declares that the German army would never leave the city of Stalingrad

509. On 31 January, newly promoted *Generalfeldmarschall* Freidrich Paulus surrendered to the Soviet Army

510. Around 91,000 German and Romanian troops were taken prisoner - only around 6,000 made it back home after the war

511. Reports on total casualties for the Battle of Stalingrad vary widely, but it estimated that the Axis forces lost anywhere between 647,000 and 968,000 men (killed, missing, wounded, captured) among all branches of their armed forces

512. Germany lost 900 aircraft (including 274 transports and 165 bombers used as transports), 500 tanks and 6,000 artillery pieces

513. According to a contemporary Soviet report, 5,762 guns, 1,312 mortars, 12,701 heavy machine guns, 156,987 rifles, 80,438 sub-machine guns, 10,722 trucks, 744 aircraft; 1,666 tanks, 261 other armoured vehicles, 571 half-tracks and 10,679 motorcycles were captured by the Soviets

514. The Soviets, according to archival figures, suffered 1,129,619 total casualties. The Axis suffered around 850,000 casualties giving a total of almost 2,000,000 for the battle of Stalingrad

515. 955 Soviet civilians died in Stalingrad and its suburbs from aerial bombing by *Luftflotte 4* as the German 4th Panzer and 6th Armies approached the city

516. During the battle of Stalingrad, conditions on the ground were so tough for Red Army soldiers and the local populace that cannibalism was a common occurrence

517. Rats also became a major source of protein for many, and horses killed in battle would usually be picked clean for meat

518. Stalingrad marked the first time that the Nazi government publicly acknowledged a failure in its war effort

519. Based on Soviet records, over 10,000 German soldiers continued to resist in isolated groups within the city for the next month

520. General Walther von Seydlitz-Kurzbach offered to raise an anti-Hitler army from the Stalingrad survivors, but the Soviets did not accept

521. 13,000 Soviet soldiers were executed at Stalingrad on grounds of desertion or cowardice in the face of the enemy

Pearl Harbor

522. The Pearl Harbor naval base was situated in Honolulu, Hawaii and was the HQ of the US Pacific Fleet

523. The Japanese used the codename *Operation Hawaii* for the attack on Pearl Harbor. This later changed to *Operation Z*

524. Plans for a surprise attack against the United States were begun as early as January of 1941 by Japanese Admiral Yamamoto Isoroku

525. In order to get into their battle positions, the Imperial Japanese fleet had to travel 4,000 miles

526. The Japanese specifically chose to attack on a Sunday because they believed Americans would be more relaxed and thus less alert on a weekend

527. The attack had several major aims. First, it intended to destroy important American fleet units, thereby preventing the Pacific Fleet from interfering with Japanese conquest of the Dutch East Indies and Malaya. Second, it was hoped to buy time for Japan to consolidate its position and increase its naval strength. Finally, it was meant to deliver a severe blow to American morale, one which would discourage Americans from committing to a war extending into the western Pacific Ocean and Dutch East Indies

528. The attack took place before any formal declaration of war was made by Japan

529. A U.S. Army private who noticed the large flight of planes on his radar screen was told to ignore them because a flight of B-17s from the mainland was expected at the time

530. The Japanese attack force was under the command of Admiral Nagumo and consisted of 6 carriers with 423 planes

531. The first wave of 83 Japanese attack planes took off at 6am when they were just 90 minutes flight time away from their target

532. The first attack commenced at 7.48am Hawaiian time on Sunday 7 December 1941

533. The whole attack lasted approximately 110 minutes

534. When Japanese Commander Mitsuo Fuchida called out, *Tora! Tora! Tora!* ("Tiger! Tiger! Tiger!") upon flying over Pearl Harbor, it was a message to the entire Japanese navy telling them they had caught the Americans totally by surprise

535. The main target of the Japanese was to be the aircraft carriers; however, since all 3 U.S. aircraft carriers were out to sea, the Japanese focused on the battleships

536. There were 8 battleships at Pearl Harbor that day, which included all the battleships of the U.S. Pacific fleet except for the *USS Colorado*

537. During the attack, the *USS Nevada* left her berth in Battleship Row and tried to make it to the harbour entrance. After being repeatedly attacked on its way, the Nevada beached itself

538. The *USS Nevada* was hit by 6 bombs and 1 torpedo. 60 crew died but she returned to service in October 1942

539. The *USS Arizona* exploded when an armour-piercing bomb breached its forward magazine (ammunition store). 1,177 U.S. servicemen died on board

540. After being hit by a total of 5 torpedoes, the *USS Oklahoma* listed so badly that she turned upside down. 429 crew were lost. She was eventually re-floated in November 1943 but capsized again while being towed to the mainland in May 1947

541. The *USS Pennsylvania* was the flagship of the US Pacific Fleet – she was in drydock at the time of the attack and was only hit by 1 bomb that resulted in minimal damage and just 9 dead. She remained in service after the attack

542. To aid their airplanes, the Japanese sent in 5 midget subs to help target the battleships. The Americans sunk 4 of the midget subs and captured the other

543. A total of 2,335 U.S. servicemen were killed and 1,143 were wounded. 68 civilians were also killed with another 35 were wounded

544. The Japanese also sank or damaged 3 cruisers, 3 destroyers, an anti-aircraft training ship, and a minelayer

545. After the *USS Arizona* sank, its superstructure and main armament were salvaged and reused to support the war effort, leaving its hull, two gun turrets and the remains of more than 1,000 crewmen submerged in less than 40 feet of water

546. *USS Arizona* was full of fuel when she was hit, nearly 1,500,000 gallons of it. To this day, the wreck still leaks fuel

547. 23 sets of brothers were killed on board the *USS Arizona*

548. In March 1961, Elvis Presley performed a benefit concert at Pearl Harbor's Block Arena that raised over $50,000 in aid of building a memorial to the *USS Arizona*

549. Many U.S. servicemen were either still in their pyjamas or eating breakfast in the mess halls when the attack on Pearl Harbor began

550. As well as attacking the ships, the Japanese struck the airfields at Hickam Field, Wheeler Field, Bellows Field, Ewa Field, Schofield Barracks, and Kaneohe Naval Air Station

551. The Japanese hoped to destroy U.S. planes on the ground in order to minimise any counter-attack against them over Pearl Harbor or against the Japanese attack force

552. Many of the U.S. airplanes were lined up outside, along the airstrips, wingtip to wingtip, in order to avoid sabotage. Unfortunately, that made them easy targets for the Japanese attackers

553. Unable to get more than a handful of planes in the air, individual U.S. servicemen tried to shoot down the Japanese planes from the ground

554. Other strategic targets at Pearl Harbour such as the oil field and the submarine base were ignored by the Japanese. They thought the war would be over before these items would be of significance

555. In the attack, 188 U.S. aircraft were destroyed

556. The midget submarine of Kazuo Sakamaki was captured intact and taken on tours of the USA to sell war bonds

557. Sakamaki became the first Japanese prisoner of war in American captivity during the war. He was subsequently erased from Japanese records and officially ceased to exist

558. Overall, Japanese losses at Pearl Harbor were light: 29 aircraft and 5 midget submarines lost, and 65 servicemen killed or wounded

559. Following the attack on Pearl Harbor, U.S. President Franklin D. Roosevelt declared that December 7, 1941 would be "a date that will live in infamy"

560. The United States declared war on Japan on 8 December 1941

561. After the attack on Pearl Harbour, the Canadians declared war on Germany before the USA did

562. Veterans of the attack have the option to join their lost comrades and make Pearl Harbor their final resting place. Crewmembers who served on board the *USS Arizona* -- which experienced the most devastating damage when the attack occurred may choose to have their ashes deposited by divers beneath one of the sunken Arizona's gun turrets

1942

563. On June 7, 1942, the German infantry launches an assault on Sebastopol, supported by as many as 1,000 *Luftwaffe* sorties a day

564. US bombers carry out their first raid over Northern Europe on 4 July 1942

565. On 19 November 1942 the Red Army launched *Operation Uranus* in an effort to cut through weak Romanian defences and encircle the German 6th Army

566. The *Luftwaffe* promised it could deliver the 700 tonnes of supplies the German Sixth Army needed each day to survive. However, it only managed to successfully deliver around 90 tonnes a day

Thousand Bomber Raids

567. The first '1000 Bomber Raid' contained 1,047 RAF bombers and took part on 30 May 1942. The target was the city of Cologne

568. The schedule of the raid allowed for just 90 minutes for all the bombers to pass over the city and release their bombs

569. Approximately 1,500 tonnes of explosives were dropped on Cologne that night - two thirds of which were incendiary bombs

570. During the raid 12,000 non-residential buildings were damaged or destroyed along with 13,000 homes destroyed and another 28,000 damaged

571. 500 Cologne residents were killed with another 5,000 injured. 45,000 people were made homeless

572. During the Cologne raid the RAF suffered just 4% losses

573. 2 more 'thousand bomber raids' were carried out. 959 bombers targeted Essen on 1 June 1942 and 1067 bombers attacked Bremen on 25 June

574. The historic cities of Bath, Exeter, Canterbury, Norwich and York were picked as targets for the *Luftwaffe* during the Spring and Summer of 1942 in retaliation for the RAF bombing of the picturesque German town of Lübeck. It is claimed the 5 cities were picked from a travel guide of England

Operation Anthropoid

575. *Operation Anthropoid* was the codename given to the plan to assassinate *SS -Obergruppenführer und General der Polizei* Reinhard Heydrich, head of the *Reichssicherheitshauptamt* (the combined security services of Nazi Germany) and acting *Reichsprotektor* of the Protectorate of Bohemia and Moravia

576. The operation was carried out by soldiers of the Czechoslovak army-in-exile, in Prague, on 27 May 1942, after preparation and training by the British Special Operations Executive and with the approval of the Czechoslovak government-in-exile

577. Preparations for the attack began on 20 October 1941 and were led by František Moravec, head of the Czechoslovak intelligence services with the knowledge and backing of the Czechoslovak government in exile in Britain

578. Moravec personally chose the men to be involved in the mission and they were all sent to a SOE commando training centre in Arisaig, Scotland

579. Originally Warrant Officer Jozef Gabčík and Staff Sergeant Karel Svoboda were chosen to carry out the operation on 28 October 1941 (Czechoslovakia's Independence Day), but Svoboda was injured during training and had to be replaced by Jan Kubiš. This delayed the mission because Kubiš had not finished his training and didn't have the necessary false documentation made up for him

580. Gabčík and Kubiš parachuted into Czechoslovakia during the night of 28/29 December 1941 and made their way to Plzen and then Prague in order to plan their attack

581. The assassination attempt took place in Prague as Heydrich was commuting from his home just north of central Prague, to his headquarters at Prague Castle

582. As Heydrich's car slowed to navigate a tight corner, Gabčík pulled out a Sten machine gun and tried to shoot Heydrich at close range. But his gun jammed. Instead of accelerating away, Heydrich ordered his driver to stop and took aim at Gabčík with his pistol. As the car came to a stop Kubiš threw a modified anti-tank grenade towards the car which landed against the rear wheel and exploded. Seriously wounding Heydrich

583. On hearing about the incident, Heinrich Himmler sent his personal physician, Karl Gebhardt to Prague to help with Heydrich's recovery

584. Gabčík and Kubiš hid in safe houses in Prague before taking refuge in the Church of Saints Cyril and Methodius in the city. The Germans were unable to find them until they were betrayed by Karel Čurda who gave information of several safe houses in return for a bounty of 1,000,000 Reichsmarks

585. On 18 June, 750 SS troops lay siege to the church. They used tear gas and even tried to flood the crypt where Gabčík and Kubiš along with other supporters were hiding. But they were unable to take any of them alive. Gabčík committed suicide and Kubiš was found unconscious and died shortly afterwards from wounds

586. After initially recovering well, Heydrich suddenly collapsed and went into a coma whilst eating a meal on 3 June. He died at around 4.30am the following day. His autopsy indicated he had died of Sepsis

587. This was the only government-sponsored assassination of a senior Nazi leader during the Second World War

588. In retaliation for the death of Heydrich, Hitler ordered that all males over the age of 16 in the Czech villages of Lidice and Ležáky were to be executed. Both towns were levelled. The women were either shot or sent to Ravensbruck concentration camp and the children were either gassed at Chelmno extermination camp or chosen for Germanisation.

589. Overall, at least 1,300 Czechs, including 200 women, were killed in reprisal for Heydrich's assassination

Africa, El Alamein and Operation Torch

590. General Bernard Montgomery was given command of the beleaguered British Eighth Army in August 1942. His appointment, along with a fresh influx of tanks and supplies greatly lifted morale of the men

591. Physically exhausted and suffering from a liver infection and low blood pressure, Rommel flew home to Germany to recover in September 1942

592. The Germans laid over 500,000 mines in huge minefields all over the desert battlefield - the British called these minefields 'The Devil's Gardens'

593. At 21:40 on 23 October *Operation Lightfoot* (the Second Battle of El-Alamein) began with a 1000-gun bombardment. Allied guns fired 529,000 shells onto German positions during a 5-hour barrage

594. For *Operation Lightfoot*, Montgomery had almost twice as many men and twice as many tanks as the Afrika Korps

595. General Georg Stumme, who took over command of the *Afrika Korps* while Rommel was in Germany, died of a heart attack on 24 October while at the front line. Rommel, still sick, was ordered to return to Africa immediately

596. By 27 October, Rommel was down to 114 German tanks and by 2 November his men had used up most of its ammunition and had only a handful tanks left. Rommel requested permission to retire, but Hitler ordered him to stand fast

597. Montgomery's Eighth Army finally broke through Axis lines on 4 November. Rommel ignored Hitler's orders and immediately ordered a retreat

598. German losses in the battle were approximately 1,100 killed, 3,900 wounded and 7,900 prisoners. Italian losses are reported to be 1,200 killed, 1,600 wounded and 20,000 prisoners

599. The Eighth Army had 13,560 casualties, of whom 2,350 men had been killed, 8,950 wounded and 2,260 were missing

600. To celebrate victory at El Alamein, church bells were rung throughout Britain - it was the first time they had rung since Dunkirk in 1940

601. On 8 November 1942 *Operation Torch* - the Allied invasion of French North Africa - commenced with 3 amphibious Task Forces tasked with occupying key ports and airports across Morocco and Algeria, areas which were under control of Vichy France

602. In total, 107,000 Allied troops were involved in *Operation Torch*

603. *Operation Torch* was the first time the British and Americans had jointly worked on an invasion plan together

604. The amphibious landings went ahead with no naval or air bombardment as it was hoped that the French troops inland would co-operate with the Allies. The French did fire back, with sniper fire being particularly problematic - but it was soon overcome

605. *Operation Torch* was a big success with all initial military targets accomplished by 10 November

The War in the Pacific

606. The Battle of the Coral Sea took place between US and Japanese navies south-east of New Guinea on 7 & 8 May 1942 and was the first naval battle to take place where the opposing ships could not see each other. Instead, the fight was carried out by aircraft

607. After 2 days, both sides had suffered heavy damage and moved out of the area. It was the first time a Japanese advance in the Pacific had been stopped

608. Almost exactly 1 month after Coral Sea the US and Japanese navies clashed again at Midway Atoll on 4 June

609. During the Battle of Midway the Japanese lost 337 aircraft - almost half of their entire carrier-based fleet

610. Japan also lost 4 aircraft carriers during the Battle of Midway - The *Akagi, Kaga, Sõryũ* and the *Hiryũ*

611. US losses at Midway were also significant: 360 men, 145 planes and 2 ships (the *USS Yorktown* and the *USS Hammann*)

612. The first Japanese bombing raid of the Australian port town of Darwin on 19 February 1942 was the largest single attack every mounted by a foreign nation upon Australian territory, with 242 enemy aircraft taking part

613. The Japanese bombed the Australian port of Darwin 64 times

614. On 11 November 1940, the German raider Atlantis captured the British steamer *Automedon* in the Indian Ocean, carrying papers meant for Air Marshal Sir Robert Brooke-Popham, the British commander in the Far East. The papers included much information regarding the strengths and weaknesses of the British base in Singapore

615. To secure vital industrial resources such as oil the Japanese started to plan to invade Malaya, Hong Kong and Singapore before moving on to the oil rich areas of the Dutch East Indies

616. The Japanese 25th Army conducted seaborne invasions of north Malaya and Thailand from their starting point in Indochina on 8 December 1941 - just 24 hours after the bombing of Pearl Harbor

617. The British had spotted the build-up of Japanese forces in Indochina a month before hand, and had drafted up plans for a pre-emptive invasion of Thailand - *Operation Matador* - however the plan was never put into action

618. Early on 8 December 1941, Singapore was bombed for the first time by long-range Japanese aircraft

619. Prior to the invasion on 8 December there were 75 Allied aircraft stationed in northern Malaya and 83 in Singapore. The Japanese had over 450 aircraft available and as such controlled the airspace over the battlefields

620. The Japanese landings on Singapore started at 20:30 on 8 December. During the night they managed to land around 13,000 troops with another 10,000 landing the following morning

621. It took the Japanese forces just 7 days to capture Singapore

622. The surrender of the British in Singapore on 15 February 1942 was the British Army's biggest ever defeat with 130,000 British, Australian, Indian and Malay troops taken prisoner

623. The Japanese advanced 600 miles in 54 days in the capture of Malaya and Singapore

624. US bombers attack Tokyo for the first time on 18 April

Burma

625. Indian troops made up the vast majority of the Allied force in Burma with 340,000 Indian soldiers and airmen deployed in the area, compared to 100,000 British forces

626. The Chindits were a special forces unit made up of British, Gurkha and Burmese soldiers led by Orde Wingate, formed to carry out long range missions deep into enemy held territory

627. The Chindits were named after the Chinthe - a mythical half lion / half dragon creature that guarded Burmese temples

628. The Burma-Thailand Railway was started after the Battle of Midway in the summer of 1942 after the Japanese Navy could no longer guarantee the safe passage of army supplies up to the Indian border

629. The railway, which would cross 420km of mountainous jungle, connected Nong Pladuk in Thailand to Thanbyuzayat in Burma. It was expected to enable the Japanese to move 3,000 tons of supplies each day from Singapore and Bangkok to the Indian border

630. In early 1942, prisoners of war started to clear undergrowth and making the cuttings - using little more than picks and shovels

631. In total some 64,000 Allied prisoners of war were forced to work on the railway

632. 12,000 Japanese soldiers, including 800 Koreans were employed on the railway as engineers and guards of the prisoners

633. 12,000 Allied prisoners died during the construction of the railway. It is estimated that another 70,000 Burmese, Malayan, Indonesian and Thai civilian workers also died

634. The Japanese transported approximately 500,000 tonnes of supplies and equipment via the railway before it fell into Allied hands

635. The cutting at Konyu was known as Hell Fire Pass. It was 500 metres long and 24 metres high. Out of the 1000 prisoners who started work on the cutting in April 1943 only 100 had survived by the time it had been completed in August

636. The railway was completed ahead of schedule on 17 October 1943

Sicily and Operation Husky

637. The Allies invade Sicily (*Operation Husky*) during the night of 9/10 July 1942

638. The initial invasion force involved in *Operation Husky* numbered 160,000 men along with 600 tanks and 14,000 other vehicles

639.   Because of strong winds on 12 out of the 144 gliders carrying British airborne troops to Sicily landed at their designated sites - half ended up in the sea

640.   In an effort to disguise the details of *Operation Husky* and confuse the enemy, an elaborate deception plan - codenamed *Operation Mincemeat* - was put into practice using the corpse of a tramp which was dressed up as an officer of the Royal Marines. This fictitious officer had documents that showed the real invasion targets were Greece and Sardinia, and that Sicily was just a diversion. Although it is unknown if the ruse really worked, decoded German messages seem to show reinforcements being ordered to Greece and Sardinia ahead of the invasion

641.   110,000 Axis troops were evacuated back to mainland Italy

1943

642. The German army officially surrendered at Stalingrad on 31 January 1943

643. *Operation Gomorrah* was the code name given to the series of bombing missions launched against the German city of Hamburg which began on 24 July and lasted for 8 days

644. 9,000 tonnes of explosives were dropped onto Hamburg during *Operation Gomorrah*. The RAF used 3,000 aircraft during the raids

645. *Operation Gomorrah* killed 38,975 people and wounded another 37,000. Almost 1,000,000 Hamburg residents were forced to flee the city

Operation Chastise (The Dambusters)

646. On the night of 16-17 May 1943, RAF Bomber Command attack 3 Ruhr Dams (the Möhne Dam, the Eder Dam and the Sorpe Dam) in the famous 'Dambuster' raid

647. The official codename given to the bombing raid on the Ruhr Dams was *Operation Chastise*

648. A special 'bouncing bomb' was developed for the mission by Dr Barnes Wallis - an employee of the Vickers Aircraft Company. The plan was for the bomb to skip across the water and smash into the wall of the dams just below water level

649. The bomb itself was codenamed 'Upkeep' and was 50 inches in diameter, 60 inches long and weighed 9,250 lbs (4,195kg)

650. At the moment of bomb release the pilots had to fly their Lancaster bombers exactly 60 feet above the water and at a steady speed of 232mph (373 km/h)

651. To add to the difficulties, the crew had to drop the bomb 425 yards from the dam wall and they were only allowed a discrepancy of 25 yards either side of this figure

652. From 9.28pm on 16 May, 133 aircrew in 19 Lancasters took off in 3 waves to bomb the dams. Squadron Leader Guy Gibson flew in the first wave - his target was the large Möhne Dam

653. Of the 133 aircrew that took part, 53 men were killed and 3 became prisoners of war

654. On the ground in Germany, almost 1,300 people were killed in the resulting flooding

655. The surviving aircrew of 617 Squadron were lauded as heroes, and Guy Gibson was awarded the Victoria Cross for his actions during the raid

656. As well as Gibson's VC, 33 other members of the raid were decorated with gallantry awards

657. After the Dams Raid, 617 Squadron made a name for itself as a precision bombing unit and often experimented with new weapons and techniques

658. Flt Sgt Leonard Sumpter, a bomb aimer, was the only man to take part in 617 Squadron's first wartime operation (the Dams Raid) and its last, an attack on Hitler's mountain lair of Berchtesgaden on 25 April 1945

Operation Citadel (Kursk)

659. The Battle of Kursk begins on 5 July 1943

660. Code named *Operation Citadel*, the Battle of Kursk was intended to smash the Red Army and prevent them from launching any new offensives for the rest of 1943. This would allow Hitler to divert his forces to the Western Front

661. British Intelligence services had provided extensive information on where a likely attack would take place. The Soviets knew months in advance that it would fall in the Kursk salient, and built up a large network of fortifications so they could defend in depth

662. It is estimated that there were as many as 6,000 tanks, 4,000 aircraft and 2 million men involved in the Battle of Kursk

663. The major clash in armour took place at Prokhorovka on 12 July when the Red Army attacked German positions with approximately 500 tanks and guns. The Soviets suffered heavy losses, but eventually won through

664. Losses at Prokhorovka were significant for both sides with Germany losing 149 tanks and the Soviets losing 412

665. Although Soviet tanks and armour were not as technologically as advanced as the Germans - they held superiority in numbers, with almost twice as many tanks available for Kursk than the Germans

666. Kursk was known for its black earth, which produced major dust clouds. These clouds hindered the *Luftwaffe's* visibility and prevented them from providing air support to soldiers on the ground

667. During the fighting at Kursk, Germany suffered 200,000 casualties from a force of 780,000 men. The attack ran out of steam after just 8 days

668. As German armour advanced at Kursk, Soviet Commander Nikolai Vatutin decided to bury his tanks so that only the top showed. This forced the German tanks closer to get a clear line of sight, eliminated the German advantage of long-range fighting, and protected Soviet tanks from direct hits

669. When Hitler received news that the Allies had invaded Sicily, he decided to cancel *Operation Citadel* and divert forces to Italy

Italy

670. Forces of the British Eighth Army landed in the 'toe' of Italy on 3 September 1943 in *Operation Baytown* - it was the same day that the Italians agreed to an armistice with the Allies

671. One of the main reasons for continuing the southern campaign onto the Italian was to occupy German forces that might otherwise be deployed to the Russian front

672. The Italians formally surrendered to the Allies on 8 September 1943

673. On 9 September, men of the US Fifth Army landed at Salerno as part of *Operation Avalanche*. To surprise the enemy, it was decided to attack without any supporting naval or air bombardment

674. As the first wave of Major General Fred Walker's U.S. 36th Infantry Division approached the Paestum shore at 03:30, a loudspeaker from the landing area proclaimed in English: "Come on in and give up. We have you covered." The Allied troops attacked nonetheless

675. As part of the reinforcements pushed in Solerno were around 1,500 men from 50th (Northumbrian) and 51st (Highland) Infantry Divisions who thought they were rejoining their old units in Sicily before returning to Britain. By the time they had arrived at Solerno they felt angry and misled and 500 veterans refused to follow orders. After being addressed by Lieutenant-General McCreery (GOC, British X Corps) all but 192 men gave in and joined new units. The 192 that were left were all charged with mutiny - it was the largest official mutiny in the history of the British Army

676. Those men accused of mutiny at Solerno were shipped off to Algeria for trial. They were all found guilty although sentences were eventually suspended

677. German forces in Italy staged a co-ordinated fighting retreat northward until they reached the heavily fortified Gustav Line which stretched along the River Garigliano to Cassino in the west and across the Apennine Mountains to Ortona on the Adriatic coast

678. Some of the heaviest defended areas of the Gustav Line was around a town called Cassino. High above the town was the 14th Century monastery of Monte Cassino - one of Italy's most important religious sites

679. There was a military exclusion zone around the monastery which both sides initially respected. The Germans did nothing more than guard the gates

680. Allied troops trying to breach the Gustav line grew very suspicious of the monastery, thinking the Germans were using it as an observation post to direct artillery fire onto Allied positions

681. Allied spotter planes wrongly identified what they thought were radio masts on the roof of the monastery and German uniforms hanging from washing lines inside the buildings - this intelligence gave way to the decision to bomb the monastery

682. The bombardment of the monastery was initially planned for 13 February, although this was changed to the 15th when severe snowstorms in the Cassino area made flying impossible

683. On the morning of the 14 February, artillery shells filled with leaflets dropped above the monastery, warning of the coming bombardment. The leaflets were dismissed as propaganda by a visiting German officer and no evacuation of the monks or refugees living in the monastery took place until it was too late

684. The following day wave upon wave of US bomber formations dropped hundreds of tonnes of explosives onto the monastery - quickly reducing it to smouldering ruin. Unfortunately, the very thing the bombardment of Monte Cassino was meant to prevent – the occupation of the abbey by German troops – was exactly what happened next. German paratroopers quickly moved into the ruins and set up strong defensive positions

685. The Battle of Monte Cassino continued for another 3 months after the bombing, the Allies suffered 55,000 casualties with the Germans losing 20,000 men

686. In order to leapfrog the Gustav Line and force open the route to Rome, the Allies developed *Operation Shingle* - an amphibious landing centred along the towns of Anzio and Nettuno, some 30 miles south of Rome on Italy's west coast

687. *Operation Shingle* was launched on 22 January 1944, just 4 days after a new US Fifth Army attack on the Garigliano and Rapido rivers near Cassino

688. Tactical surprise had been achieved and the landings were virtually unopposed. By the end of the day 36,000 troops and 3,200 vehicles had been delivered ashore with the loss of only 13 killed and 97 wounded

689. Instead of pressing on, the Allies dug in and consolidated their positions, giving the Germans time to react. By 25 January 40,000 German troops had surrounded the Allied beachhead and were ready for a counter-attack

690. The Germans also amassed huge amounts of artillery to smash the beachhead including a massive 280mm railway gun which was nicknamed 'Anzio Annie'

691. On 30 January, the Allies attempted a dual-pronged offensive aimed at capturing vital road junctions and improved defensive positions. On the right flank, 2 battalions of US Rangers were ambushed whilst attempting to capture the town of Cisterna. Only 6 out of 767 men returned

692. On the left flank the British 1st Division advanced slowly but also suffered huge casualties. The Sherwood Foresters, leading the attack, took 70% casualties and lost all their officers

693. Approximately 2,500 Allied aircraft were available to protect the bridgehead, provide close air support and disrupt enemy troop movements and communications

694. The Germans launched a second counterattack, *Operation Fischfang*, on 16 February. The main thrust was directed against the US 45th Division, with diversionary attacks around the rest of the beachhead perimeter

695. During this counter-attack the Germans deployed a number of new weapons, including *PzKpfw V Panther* tanks and Borgward remote-controlled demolition vehicles, which were particularly ineffective and became bogged down in the muddy conditions

696. After 6 weeks of intense fighting, the Anzio campaign had reached a bloody stalemate. The Germans had contained the Allied invasion force but lacked the strength to push it back into the sea. Kesselring ordered a new defence line be prepared south of Rome – the 'Caesar Line'

697. On 11 May 1944, British and US forces launched *Operation Diadem* and finally broke through at Cassino and along the Garigliano river

698. On 25 May Allied troops advancing from Anzio finally linked up with troops coming up from the Gustav Line

699. The 4-month Anzio campaign was characterised by trench warfare and artillery barrages more commonly associated with the First World War

700. American forces entered Rome in triumph on 5 June - the bulk of the German forces in the area had been pulled to the north of the city to form a new defensive line - the Gothic Line

701. Although the capture of Rome did make headlines, it was soon outshone by the launch of *Operation Overlord* and the D-Day landings which took place the very next day

702. Polish troops played a significant part in the battle of Italy although one of their ranks stood out from the crowd. Wojtek was a brown bear that had been adopted by a Polish artillery unit whilst in the Middle East and was formally enlisted into the army so he could move with them to Italy, where he helped move supplies. After the war he was moved to Edinburgh Zoo

703. It is estimated that between September 1943 and April 1945, 60,000–70,000 Allied and 38,805–150,660 German soldiers died in Italy

704. Men who fought in the Italian campaign during 1944 were known as D-Day Dodgers by those who took part in *Operation Overlord*

705. Approximately 250,000 Axis soldiers surrendered after the Allies took control of Tunis on 12 May 1943 - effectively ending the Africa campaign

1944

706. It is estimated that German armament production was reduced by 11% in 1944 due to Allied bombing raids

707. During a night raid on Nuremberg on the 30 March 1944, Bomber Command lost 95 out of a total of 795 aircraft in what was to be their costliest mission of the war. 545 aircrew were killed

708. In May of 1944, the Luftwaffe suffered 50% losses amongst its fighters

The Atlantic Wall

709. The Commander in Chief of the German army in the West was Field Marshal Gerd von Rundstedt

710. Von Rundstedt had 850,000 men at his disposal, plus the Atlantic Wall

711. The Atlantic Wall were coastal defences that ran from Norway to the Franco-Spanish border

712. In 1944, Erwin Rommel began to take charge of the Atlantic Wall

713. Over 1,200,000 tonnes of steel and 17,000,000 cubic metres of concrete were used in building the Atlantic Wall

714. The Atlantic Wall included 92 manned radar sites

715. By summer 1944 over 5,000,000 sea mines had been laid along the western coast of France in anticipation of an Allied seaborne invasion

716. 260,000 workers helped to build the Atlantic Wall

717. Only 10% of these were German

718. Hitler wanted 15,000 concrete strong points to be manned by 300,000 troops. Ultimately though, this would prove to be impossible to achieve

D-Day & Operation Overlord

719. The "D" is derived from the word "Day". "D-Day" means the day on which a military operation begins. The term "D-Day" has been used for many different operations, but it is now generally only used to refer to the Allied landings in Normandy on 6 June 1944

720. In October 1941 Winston Churchill told Captain Lord Louis Mountbatten to start thinking about an invasion of Europe: "Unless we can go on land and fight Hitler and beat his forces on land, we shall never win this war"

721. Lt-General Sir Frederick Morgan was appointed Chief of Staff to the Supreme Allied Commander (COSSAC) and in April 1943 was told to prepare for a '...full scale assault against the continent...'

722. On 7 December 1943 President Roosevelt met with US General Dwight D. Eisenhower in Tunis and told him he would be commanding the invasion

723. Eisenhower was put in charge of SHAEF (Supreme Headquarters Allied Expeditionary Force) and started work on coordinating and carrying out the Normandy landings

724. All information pertaining to the invasion were marked 'Bigot'. A classification even more secret than 'Top Secret'

725. D-Day was originally set for 5 June but was delayed 24 hours due to poor weather

726. In the months running up to D-Day, Eisenhower smoked up to 4 packets of Camel cigarettes a day

727. In the preparation and execution of D-Day around 17,000,000 maps were drawn up

728. *Operation Tonga* was the codename given to the airborne operation undertaken by the British 6th Airborne Division between 5 June and 7 June 1944 as a part of *Operation Overlord* and the D-Day landings

729. *Operation Tonga* had 3 main objectives: Capturing the two bridges crossing the Orne river and the Caen canal (*Operation Deadstick*); silencing the Merville Battery and the destruction of 5 bridges east of the Orne river to disrupt any German counter-attack

730. Some 8,500 men took part in *Operation Tonga*

731. *Operation Deadstick* was the name given to the glider operation to capture 2 small bridges that crossed the Caen Canal and the Orne River near the town of Bénouville. Capturing these bridges would mean the enemy would have a 6-hour detour through the centre of Caen to get to the beach zones

732. *Operation Deadstick* was carried out by 'D' Company, 2nd Airborne Battalion, Oxfordshire and Buckinghamshire Light Infantry under the command of Major John Howard

733. By 00:21 the 3 glider crews had captured the Bénouville canal bridge intact had nullified all German resistance in the vicinity. It had taken just 10 minutes

734. Lieutenant Herbert Denham Brotheridge was killed by machine-gun fire during the capture of the bridge and is widely recognised as being the first Allied soldier killed by enemy action on D-Day, 6 June 1944

735. The River bridge was taken without a shot being fired

736. Of the 181 men (139 infantry, 30 engineers and 12 pilots) of 'D' Company involved in the capture of the bridges, 2 were killed and an additional 14 wounded

737. The Caen Canal bridge was renamed Pegasus Bridge after the emblem of the British airborne forces, while the River Orne bridge became Horsa Bridge

738. Heavy cloud, a lack of navigators and enemy anti-aircraft fire meant that many men were dropped in the wrong place. It is estimated that no more than 60% of the men dropped took any active part in the day's action

739. The 6th Airborne Division suffered a total of 800 casualties between 5 - 7 June

740. British Paratroopers entered the Café Gondrée on the west bank of the Caen canal at 06:20 on D-Day, making it the first building to be liberated by Allied troops

741. Almost 6,000 men of the 101st US Airborne and 6,500 men from the 82nd US Airborne were dropped over the western flank of the invasion beaches in the early hours of D-Day

742. The 101st Airborne suffered 182 men killed with another 557 wounded and 501 taken prisoner

743. The 82nd Airborne suffered 156 men killed with 347 wounded and 756 taken prisoner

744. The deception plan to keep the Germans guessing as to when/where the invasion would take place was called Operation Bodyguard

745. To help the Allies there were around 350,000 Resistance members in France

746. Only 100,000 Resistance members had working weapons

747. Major General Percy Hobart devised several specialist vehicles for the invasion, including armoured bulldozers and swimming tanks. They were nicknamed 'Hobart's Funnies'

748. Around 30,000 practice launches for the swimming tanks were undertaken

749. Designed to aid recognition, all Allied aircraft except for readily identifiable heavy bombers and seaplanes were required to wear invasion stripes on their wings and fuselage

750. Between January and June 1944, British factories produced 7,000,000 jerry cans in preparation for the invasion

751. During practise landings on Slapton Sands 946 Allied soldiers were killed due to an attack by German E-boats

752. The Allied invasion force sailed to a rendezvous area in the middle of the Channel nicknamed 'Piccadilly Circus'. From there they would sail to the invasion zones

753. Before anyone had set foot on the beaches on 6 June, Bomber Command had already lost 300 aircraft and over 2,000 personnel attacking invasion targets in the run up to D-Day

754. The seaborne assault phase of *Operation Overlord* was called *Operation Neptune*

755. 195,700 Personnel were involved in *Operation Neptune*. 52,889 Americans, 112,824 British and 4,988 from other countries

756. 6,939 vessels were used during *Operation Neptune* including 1,213 naval warships and 4,126 landing ships and crafts

757. On top of this, 11,590 aircraft were available to support the initial invasion

758. The oldest Allied battleship in action on D-Day was the *USS Arkansas*. She was commissioned in 1912

759. At 05:23 on 6 June, *HMS Warspite* fired the opening salvo of the naval bombardment that would precede the invasion

760. 73,000 US troops and 83,000 British and Canadian troops crossed the channel on D-Day

761. All American service personnel were required to take out a $10,000 life insurance policy

762. The crossing took around 17 hours

763. The LST (Landing Ship Tank) could carry 20 tanks, 400 battle ready troops or 2,100 tonnes of supplies

764. Modified LCT's were able to fire rockets. These LCT(R)'s fired over 14,000 rockets on D-Day

765. 13,348 Paratroopers were dropped inland from the invasion beaches 5 hours before the coastal landings

766. Just 1 in 6 Allied paratroopers landed in the correct place

767. The Germans had a number of remote control 'Goliath' tanks that each carried 224 pounds of explosives

768. Allied aircraft dropped 7,200,000 pounds of bombs on D-Day

769. No Allied planes were lost to the *Luftwaffe* on D-Day. Although 113 were shot down by anti-aircraft fire

770. There were to be 5 invasion beaches: Utah, Omaha, Gold, Juno and Sword

771. During D-Day 2,240 SAS troops were dropped across the French coastline. Their job was to divert attention from the real invasion areas

772. On Utah beach the men of the first assault wave had just a 50/50 chance of survival

773. Overlooking Utah beach, the Germans had 110 artillery pieces, with another 18 large batteries situated inland

774. In the end, Utah beach saw a successful landing with 20,000 men put ashore with just 300 casualties

775. On Omaha Beach 'A' Company of the US 116th Infantry Regiment lost 96% of its effective strength in one hour

776. There were 2,400 casualties on Omaha on D-Day, out of a total of 34,000 men who came ashore

1001 Sensational Second World War Facts

777. When the US Rangers climbed to the top of Pointe du Hoc they found the German guns were not there

778. The British landed 24,970 troops on Gold beach with 400 casualties

779. On Juno Beach the Canadians suffered 1,200 casualties but also managed to advance up to 6 miles inland

780. On Sword beach 28,845 men were set ashore with just 630 casualties

781. 21% of Allied wounded on D-Day were operated on within an hour

782. On D-Day, 5,656 RAF aircraft were involved in some way or another

783. During the Battle for Normandy, the RAF flew over 225,000 sorties

784. 1,800 RAF personnel and 456 RAF vehicles landed ashore on D-Day

785. By 9 June, 3,500 RAF personnel and 815 vehicles had landed in Normandy, working on airfield construction, servicing and forward controlling

786. 2 temporary harbours called 'Mulberry's' were built to unload supplies

787. In the first few weeks after D-Day RAF Bomber Command averaged 5,000 sorties per week across Normandy

788. In order to continue supplying fuel to the invasion armies a PipeLine Under The Ocean (PLUTO) was laid that delivered Allied fuel directly to France

789. Only Hitler could order the Panzers to move out and counter-attack the invasion. He slept through until midday on D-Day

790. The town of Bedford, Virginia suffered the highest per capita loss of any US community on D-Day with 19 men killed. It was later chosen as the site of the US National D-Day Memorial

791. Ranville was the first French village to be liberated as part of *Operation Overlord* by the 13th (South Lancashire) Parachute Battalion at around 02:30 on D-Day

792. Lt Colonel Terence Otway of the 9th Battalion, Parachute Regiment was given the task of leading the attack on the formidable Merville gun battery. As part of the plan he was to have 750 men but only 150 made it to the rendezvous position in time for the attack

793. 5 Gliders carrying vital equipment for the Merville assault were lost at sea en route to the battery

794. *Operation Titanic* was the name given to a series of parachute drop deceptions carried out during the early hours of D-Day. Members of the SAS and hundreds of dummy parachutists called 'Ruperts' were dropped deep inland behind the beaches to confuse the enemy as to the exact details of the invasion

795. The 'Ruperts' were crude dummies made of sand, straw and fabric. Each one had a parachute and carried an incendiary device which would fire on landing, removing any evidence that they were not real paratroopers

Valkyrie

796. On 20 July 1944 Hitler survives *Operation Valkyrie* - an assassination attempt led by Claus von Stauffenberg inside the Wolf's Lair

797. Out of the 24 people present in the Wolf's Lair conference room when the bomb went off, 4 people were killed with the other 20 suffering varying injuries

798. Hitler himself suffered burns, a busted eardrum and temporary paralysis of an arm

799. Following the failed assassination attempt the Gestapo arrested around 7,000 people and executed 4,980 of them. Not everyone was directly linked with the assassination attempt - the Gestapo used the situation as an excuse to settle numerous old scores

800. As a result of the failed coup, every member of the *Wehrmacht* was required to re-swear his loyalty oath, by name, to Hitler and, on 24 July 1944, the military salute was replaced throughout the armed forces with the Hitler Salute in which the arm was outstretched and the salutation Heil Hitler was given

Antwerp

801. The port of Antwerp fell into Allied hands on 4 September 1944

802. During the breakout into the city of Antwerp the Allies took around 5,000 German prisoners - they were all kept in the city's zoo

803. On 11 September the first Allied troops walked on German soil when a small US group from the 85th Reconnaissance Squadron (5th Armored Division) crossed the River Our on the border of Luxembourg and Germany and entered the German hamlet of Gmuend. After making their small piece of history they quickly returned - encountering no enemy resistance

Operation Bagration

804. *Operation Bagration*, the great Soviet offensive of 1944, was launched on 22 June with a force of 1,670,000 men

805. With more than 2,300,000 men involved over the course of the attack, 6 times the artillery and twice the number of tanks that launched the Battle of the Bulge, it was the largest Allied operation of the war

806. *Operation Bagration* was preceded by coordinated partisan attacks on German supply lines, code-named "Rail War" and "Concert." Between 19/23 June 19 Belorussian guerrillas sabotaged rail networks and bridges — detonating some 10,500 demolition charges during the night of June 19/20 alone — impeding the movement of ammunition, food, and reinforcements to the front

807. Originally timed for 14 June 1944, the operation's start was delayed by Soviet rail congestion until 22 June 1944 — 3 years to the day from the Nazi invasion of Soviet territory

808. For the opening bombardment, each Russian artillery gun along the line was allotted roughly 6 tons of ammunition to fire during 2-hour barrage

809. During the night of 22/23 June, Soviet bombers flew over 1,000 sorties softening up German strong points and defensive networks

810. In 4 weeks, *Operation Bagration* inflicted greater losses on the German army than the Wehrmacht had suffered in 5 months at Stalingrad

811. Exact German casualties are unknown, but estimates suggest between 350,000 - 400,000 total casualties

812. 57,000 German prisoners were transported to Moscow and paraded before the locals on 17 July. Despite marching quickly and 20 abreast, the parade took 90 minutes

813. By mid-August, Soviet troops were digging in on Prussian soil and just 350 miles from Berlin. 30 German infantry divisions had been destroyed with another 30 on the brink of destruction. But the Soviets were exhausted too and had to stop their advance

814. By 1945 the Soviet could call on over 6,000,000 troops, whilst German strength had been reduced to less than a third of this

815. When allied armies reached the Rhine, the first thing men did was pee in it. This was universal from the lowest private to Winston Churchill (who made a big show of it) and Gen. Patton (who had himself photographed in the act)

816. The first concentration camp to be liberated was the Majdanek Camp in Poland which was reached by the Russians on 22 July 1944. The Germans had already left the camp and had destroyed most of it - although the crematoria remained

817. By June 1944, the *Luftwaffe* were outnumbered over 30:1 in the west

818. The Allies invade the south of France on 15 August

819. Paris was liberated on 25 August

Operation Market Garden

820. *Operation Market Garden* was the name given to the Allied military operation in the Netherlands that occurred between 17 and 25 September 1944. The plan was centred around Allied airborne units seizing the main bridges across the lower Rhine and its neighbouring rivers/tributaries and holding them long enough for Allied armoured divisions to reach them. From there, the Allies could strike into the heartlands of the Third Reich

821. *Operation Market Garden* was the brainchild of General Montgomery and started on 17 September

822. There were 2 parts to *Operation Market Garden*. *Operation Market* was the landing of 40,000 paratroopers behind enemy lines to take control of the bridges and hold them long enough for the tanks to cross. *Operation Garden* involved the advance of a British tank and mobile infantry force across the bridges and on into Germany

823. The airborne divisions involved in *Operation Market* were the 101st US Airborne Division, the 82nd US Airborne Division, the British 1st Airborne Division and the 1st Polish Independent Airborne Brigade

824. The 101st Airborne had to capture 5 bridges near Eindhoven on the first day of the operation. The British at Arnhem had 2 bridges to take, the most important being the road bridge. The 82nd US Airborne were tasked in capturing the Waal Bridge at Nijmegen

825. The bridges, however, were not the final target of the Operation. Whilst a section of the Allied force would keep the bridges secure, the rest would press on to the north to capture the *Luftwaffe* airfield at Deelen before going further north to Zuiderzee

826. Dutch resistance groups cautioned the Allies against the plan - insisting that the German army was not as beaten as the Allies thought they were

827. The RAF refused to drop the British closer than 8 miles from Arnhem because they feared suffering heavy losses from anti-aircraft fire

828. An SS training battalion happened to be training in the woods near the British drop zone. They reacted quickly to the invasion and managed to mount a strong defensive action

829. Although much of the British Airborne division never reached the town, Arnhem Bridge was captured, and the men defiantly resisted German attacks for 3 days before being overwhelmed

830. The Germans destroyed 2 of the 5 bridges before the 101st Airborne were able to capture them

831. James Gavin, the 6th Airborne commander, could only send 1 battalion to capture the Nijmegen bridge, which was heavily defended. The rest of his men were ordered to occupy the Groesbeek Heights to the southeast of the city

832. On 20 September, U.S. paratroopers crossed the River Waal in 26 small, canvas boats under heavy fire. When they reached the far side, they seized the north side of the bridge. The daring feat is regarded as among the most heroic of the entire war

The Battle of the Bulge

833. The Battle of the Bulge was the last major German counter-attack of the war and began on 16 December 1944 lasting for 6 weeks before coming to an end on 25 January 1945

834. The German counter-attack did come as a surprise to the Allies who were heavily focussed on offensive preparations and did not anticipate a major attack by Germany. Heavy fog had grounded air reconnaissance, meaning the build-up of German forces was not detected

835. The Germans attacked through the wooded Ardennes region - their target was the Belgian city of Antwerp

836. German forces for the Battle of the Bulge were almost 250,000 - against just 80,000 Allies

837. The Battle of the Bulge was the biggest battle of the Western Front and the largest engagement ever fought by the United States Army with over 600,000 GI's involved

838. The Battle of the Bulge is the second deadliest battle in American military history. US forces suffered 75,000 casualties including as many as 20,000 dead. It is only surpassed by the Meuse-Argonne Offensive of the First World War, in which more than 25,000 American soldiers were killed

839. Antwerp was targeted by V2 rockets from mid-1944 onwards. During the Battle of the Bulge, over 3700 Belgian civilians were killed in rocket attacks. On the first day of the battle, a V2 rocket hit a cinema in the city, killing 567 people

840. The Germans set aside nearly 5,000,000 gallons of fuel for the Battle of the Bulge, yet once combat operations began, poor road conditions and logistical issues ensured that much of the fuel never reached those who needed it

841. German forces became so critically short of fuel they were forced to use 50,000 horses for transport

842. 22 German commandos led by Otto Skorzeny passed into Allied territory driving American jeeps. Their job was to spread confusion and conduct sabotage operations

843. An SS unit under Joachim Peiper was responsible for a series of atrocities during the Battle of the Bulge including the Malmedy Massacre when 72 captured American soldiers were murdered on 17 December. "Avenge Malmedy" became a battle cry for American forces and 4 days later 21 German soldiers attempting to surrender were killed in an act of revenge

844. German forces had achieved an advance of less than 60 miles at its furthest point. They never reached closer than 70 miles from Antwerp

845. During the defence of Bastogne, the all-black 969th Field Artillery Battalion was awarded a Distinguished Unit Citation—the first ever presented to a black outfit

The Battle of Leyte Gulf

846. Taking place over 100,000 square miles of ocean, the Battle of Leyte Gulf is widely recognised as the largest naval battle ever fought

847. The battle involved more than 800 ships and over 2,000 aircraft

848. The battle of Leyte Gulf was actually composed of 4 separate engagements that took place between 23-26 October 1944: The Battle of the Sibuyan Sea, the Battle of Surigao Strait, the Battle of Cape Engaño and the Battle off Samar. All of these battles were fought by the US Navy's 3rd and 7th fleets against the Japanese Imperial Navy to support General Douglas MacArthur and the Allied forces in the invasion of Leyte

849. The battle of Leyte Gulf was the first battle in which the Japanese undertook co-ordinated *Kamikaze* attacks. It was also the last naval duel between battleships

850. The US lost 7 ships sunk and the Japanese lost 26 ships sunk (including the *Musashi* - the former flagship of the Japanese combined fleet) during the battle of Leyte Gulf

851. Although exact casualty numbers are impossible to ascertain it is estimated that the US Navy suffered around 3,000 casualties and the Imperial Japanese Navy suffered around 12,500 casualties

852. The amphibious invasion of the island of Leyte by members of the US Sixth Army on 20 October 1944 launched the campaign to liberate all of the Philippines from Imperial Japanese occupation

853. After 4 hours of heavy naval bombardment, men of the US Sixth Army landed on their designated beaches from 10am. Within a couple of hours most beaches were secure

854. At 1.30pm on the 20th General MacArther waded ashore and proclaimed to the Philippine people "People of the Philippines, I have returned! By the grace of Almighty God, our forces stand again on Philippine soil."

855. The Japanese had 432,000 troops in the Philippines and quickly organised a counter-attack, strafing the US invasion by air and by sea

856. MacArthur announced the control of Leyte on Christmas Day 1944 although the Japanese continued to fight until the end of the year

1945

857. On 5 May 1945, Troops of the 23rd US Tank Battalion under Captain John 'Jack' Lee and a number of German soldiers led by Major Josef 'Sepp' Gangl joined together to defend Castle Itter in Austria and its prisoners (including former French Prime Ministers and the sister of Charles de Gaulle) from the 17th *SS Panzergrenadier Division*. It is the only known time during the war that German and Americans fought side by side.

858. For his role in defending the castle, Captain Lee was awarded the Distinguished Service Cross. Major Gangl was killed by a sniper while trying to get former French Prime Minister Paul Reynaud to safety. He was the only fatality of the battle

859. When the Red Army marched into Germany, the retreating Germans openly left large amounts of alcohol as they withdrew, presuming that the Red Army would be defenceless in the face of all this free booze and hoping it would greatly reduce their effectiveness in battle

860. The US launched an amphibious assault on Luzon, the largest island in the Philippines on 9 January 1945. 175,000 men of the US 6th Army landed along a 20-mile (32 km) beachhead within a few days, with more landings taking place over the following days

861. The US had taken control of all strategically important positions across Luzon by early March - although pockets of Japanese defenders held out in the mountains until the end of the war

862. US casualties were 8,310 dead and almost 30,000 wounded however Japanese casualties were enormous - over 200,000 killed and 9,000 taken prisoner - making it the costliest battle the US were involved in throughout the entire war

863. *Operation Meetinghouse*, the US firebombing of Tokyo on 9 March 1945, is considered the deadliest bombing raid in history. A napalm attack carried out by 334 B-29 bombers; Meetinghouse killed more than 100,000 people. Several times that number were also injured

864. The total number of prisoners taken on the Western Front in April 1945 by the Western Allies was 1,500,000

865. In the 3-4 months up to the end of April, over 800,000 German soldiers surrendered on the Eastern Front

866. On 25 April 1945, Italian partisans liberated Milan and Turin. On 27 April 1945, as Allied forces closed in on Milan, Italian dictator Benito Mussolini was captured by Italian partisans. He was executed the next day and his body, along with other fascists that were also killed, was taken to Milan and hung up on the Piazzale Loreto

867. On 29 April, the day before Hitler died, *Oberstleutnant* Schweinitz and *Sturmbannführer* Wenner signed a surrender document at Caserta on behalf of *Generaloberst* Heinrich von Vietinghoff and *SS-Obergruppenführer* Karl Wolff after secret negotiations with the Western Allies. In the document, the Germans agreed to a ceasefire and surrender of all the forces under the command of Vietinghoff

868. As a consequence of the Caserta agreement, nearly 1,000,000 men in Italy and Austria surrendered unconditionally to British Field Marshal Sir Harold Alexander at 2pm on 2 May.

The Battle for Berlin

869. As Allied forces closed in on Berlin, Eisenhower had persuaded Stalin to link up their forces at Dresden before advancing on the German capital

870. As the Red Army approached Berlin, Stalin forgot all about the agreement with Eisenhower and ordered 2 rival field marshals, Konev and Zhukov, to advance directly on Berlin

871. By 15 April, American forces crossed the Elbe and were in touching distance of Berlin, but Eisenhower pulled them back and ordered them to wait for the link up with the Soviets at Dresden. The next morning Soviet Field Marshall Zhukov began his attack on Berlin

872. Propaganda minister Goebbels labelled the city "Fortress Berlin", but it was not much of a fortress. Its defenders were 90,000 children of the Hitler Youth and old men of the *Volkssturm*, Germany's equivalent of the Home Guard

873. The Red Army was not the only one participating in the Battle of Berlin. It was backed up by the 200,000-strong 1st Polish Army, which accounted for about 10 percent of all the advancing troops

874. In late April 1945, the German 12th Army launched a last-ditch attack at the Soviet forces encircling Berlin to try and create a breakthrough and a safe escape route west for trapped soldiers and civilians. Codenamed *Operation Potsdam*, it was the last full-scale German offensive of the war

875. Even the Soviet Navy took an active part in the battle for the city. From 23 to 25 April, under enemy fire, small boats of the Dnieper Flotilla transported more than 16,000 soldiers and 100 pieces of artillery by river directly into the combat area

876. When Russian troops began to move into Berlin, the first government building that took control of was the *Gestapo* HQ

877. The *Reichstag* was not captured at the first attempt. An assault on April 29 had failed, and the building was seized only by the evening of April 30

878. As the Red Army were closing in on his bunker, Adolf Hitler and his now wife, Eva Braun, both committed suicide on 30 April. Their bodies were burnt close to the bunker

879. An estimated 200,000 Germans and 150,000 Russians died in the fall of Berlin

880. As set out in his Last Will and Testament, Hitler appointed Admiral Karl Dönitz as *Reichspräsident* or "President" of the country. Joseph Goebbels was appointed as the new *Reichskanzler* or Chancellor of Germany

881. On 1 May, Joseph Goebbels and his wife Magda poisoned their 6 young children before committing suicide themselves

882. The Battle of Berlin ended on 2 May. On that date, *General der Artillerie* Helmuth Weidling, the commander of the Berlin Defence Area, unconditionally surrendered the city to General Vasily Chuikov of the Red Army

883. On 4 May 1945, British Field Marshal Bernard Montgomery took the unconditional military surrender at Lüneburg from *Generaladmiral* Hans-Georg von Friedeburg, and General Eberhard Kinzel, of all German forces in Holland, northwest Germany and Denmark. In total this amounted to around 1,000,000 men

884. On 5 May, *Großadmiral* Dönitz ordered all U-boats to cease offensive operations and return to their bases

885. On 6 May, Hermann Göring surrendered to General Carl Spaatz, commander of the operational United States Air Forces in Europe

886. At 02:41 on the morning of 7 May, at SHAEF headquarters in Reims, France, the Chief-of-Staff of the German Armed Forces High Command, General Alfred Jodl, signed an unconditional surrender document for all German forces to the Allies

887. Stalin didn't accept the Reims agreement, declaring that any surrender document should be signed in Berlin with suitable Soviet representation. Therefore, another surrender document was prepared in Moscow. Field Marshall Keitel travelled to Berlin and signed a second surrender document in the presence of Marshal Zhukov for the Soviet Union, Air Chief Marshal Arthur Tedder for the British Empire, General Carl Spaatz for the USA and General de Lattre de Tassigny for France. The signing ceremony took place in a former German Army Engineering School in the district of Karlshorst

888. There were 3 language versions of the surrender document – Russian, English, and German – with the Russian and English versions proclaimed, in the text itself, as the only authoritative ones

889. The war in Europe officially ended on 8 May 1945 (Which we now called VE Day - 'Victory in Europe')

890. At 10:00 on 8 May, the Channel Islanders were informed by the German authorities that the war was over

891. The last battle in Europe, the Battle of Odžak between the Yugoslav Army and the Croatian Armed Forces, began on 19 April 1945 and concluded on 25 May, 17 days after the surrender of Germany

892. While in captivity at Nuremberg, Göring undertook an IQ test and registered a score of 138

Okinawa & Iwo Jima

893. The Battle of Okinawa began on Easter Sunday 1945 and raged for 2 months, finally coming to an end on 22 June

894. Okinawa would be the last major battle of the Pacific and was given the code-name *Operation Iceberg*

895. *Operation Iceberg* was the largest amphibious landing in the Pacific theatre throughout the whole of the war

896. The invasion was launched on 1 April 1945, when a contingent of U.S. ground troops landed at Hagushi, on the west coast of central Okinawa. By nightfall, some 50,000 men of the U.S. 10th Army had gone ashore and established a beachhead

897. The first major Japanese counterattack came on 6-7 April in the form of suicidal raids by more than 350 *Kamikaze* planes and the battleship *Yamato*. The Japanese had hoped that the *Yamato* might finish off the Allied fleet after it had been weakened by the wave of *Kamikazes*

898. The *Yamato* tried to engage the US Fleet but with no air cover was a sitting duck for US Carrier based planes. The *Yamato* was sunk on 7 April

899. Okinawa was strategically important as it was the gateway to the mainland of Japan and would make any land-invasion of Japan much easier. In addition, the island held a critical Japanese airbase which was important to neutralise

900. The US Army fired 29,810,953 rifle and machine-gun rounds at Okinawa

901. The Japanese battleship the *Yamato* and her sistership the *Musashi* were the biggest battleships ever built, weighing 72,000 tonnes when fully loaded - 20,000 tonnes more than the *Tirpitz*

902. The Allies lost 402 ships sunk or severely damaged at Okinawa

903. At Okinawa, the Japanese unleashed the full force of *Kamikaze* - at times they launched 300 attacks a day. 1,900 Japanese pilots died

904. Dubbed "the Typhoon of Steel" for its ferocity, Okinawa was one of the bloodiest in the Pacific War, claiming the lives of 12,281 Americans and around 100,000 Japanese, including the commanding generals on both sides

905. Of the 12,281 Americans reported killed in the Okinawa campaign, 4,907 were U.S. Navy personnel

906. The civilian population of Okinawa was reduced by perhaps one quarter; 100,000 Okinawan men, women, and children perished in the fighting or committed suicide under orders from the Japanese

907. From 4 April to 26 May, U.S. forces on southern Okinawa had advanced only 4 miles

908. There were more than 110,000 Japanese killed at Okinawa

909. Around 400 Navajo Indians were employed within the US Military as 'Code Talkers' in the Pacific to help communicate important messages within the US military network. Their native language did not include words to explain much of the new military technology, so they used descriptive words instead. Submarines were called 'iron fish' and fighter planes were known as 'hummingbirds'

910. Some Navajo code talkers were mistaken for the enemy and captured by other American soldiers. To help protect them from their own side, the Code Talkers were often assigned bodyguards

911. At the Battle of Iwo Jima, Major Howard Connor, 5th Marine Division signal officer, had 6 Navajo code talkers working around the clock during the first 2 days of the battle. These 6 sent and received over 800 messages, all without error. Connor later stated, "Were it not for the Navajos, the Marines would never have taken Iwo Jima"

912. The Navajo code is the only spoken military code never to have been deciphered

913. The island of Iwo Jima has an area of just 8 square miles

914. The invasion of Iwo Jima saw US forces outnumber the Japanese by more than 3 to 1 with 70,000 US combatants up against 22,000 Japanese defenders

915. The Japanese defence was commanded by Lieutenant General Tadamichi Kuribayashi - his tactics were to to hang back and defend from deeper positions, deliberately delaying the Americans and inflicting as many casualties as possible. By doing this he hoped to break US morale and send them packing

916. Kuribayashi's deep defence strategy involved the construction of 11 miles of fortified tunnels that connected 1,500 rooms, artillery emplacements, bunkers, ammunition dumps and pillboxes

917. Ahead of the invasion the US launched a 3-day bombardment, but it had limited impact due to the Japanese troops being largely underground

918. Once the landings were underway the Japanese hardly fired a shot in anger at the amassing US troops on the beaches. This did nothing but lull the Americans into a false sense of security. Only once the beach was full of men and equipment did Kuribayashi allow his heavy artillery to smash the landing zones from all angles

919. The M2 flamethrower was considered to be the single most effective weapon for the Americans in the Iwo Jima engagement and it quickly became the go-to weapon for clearing enemy held bunkers, caves and fortifications

920. Over the course of the 36-day engagement there were at least 26,000 US casualties, including 6,800 dead. This made Iwo Jima the only battle of the Pacific War in which American casualties outnumbered Japanese

921. The ferocity of the fighting at Iwo Jima led to 22 US Marines and 5 members of the US Navy being awarded a Medal of Honor

922. The iconic image of the taking of Mount Suribachi was captured by Joe Rosenthal on 23 February 1945

923. The Battle for Iwo Jima ended on 25 March 1945. There was no significant tactical advantage in capturing the island, the airfields were rebuilt, and the island was used as an emergency landing area for the USAAF

Hiroshima & Nagasaki

924. On August 6, 1945, an American B-29 bomber dubbed Enola Gay dropped an atomic bomb on the Japanese city of Hiroshima. It was the first time a nuclear weapon had been deployed in warfare and the bomb immediately killed 80,000 people. Tens of thousands more would later die of radiation exposure

925. Nagasaki was hit with a second Atomic Bomb on 9 August

926. There were 5 Japanese cities on the US's initial hit list and Nagasaki was not one of them. The list included Kokura, Hiroshima, Yokohama, Niigata and Kyoto. It's said that Kyoto was ultimately spared because US Secretary of War Henry Stimson was fond of the ancient Japanese capital, having spent his honeymoon there decades earlier. Nagasaki took its place instead

927. The bomb that was dropped on Hiroshima was called 'Little Boy' and was made of highly enriched uranium-235

928. The bomb that was dropped on Nagasaki was called 'Fat Man' and was made of plutonium

929. The bombs' codenames were chosen by their creator Robert Serber, who apparently drew inspiration from John Huston's 1941 film The Maltese Falcon

930. Before the atomic attacks, the US Air Force dropped pamphlets in Japan which promised "prompt and utter destruction" and urged civilians to flee

931. The bomb blast in Hiroshima was of such intensity that it permanently burned the shadows of people and objects into the ground. These became known as "Hiroshima shadows"

932. The official flower of the city of Hiroshima is the oleander - it was the first plant to blossom again after the atomic bomb blast

933. In Hiroshima's Peace Memorial Park, a flame has burned continuously since it was lit in 1964. The "Peace Flame" will remain lit until all nuclear bombs on the planet are destroyed and the planet is free from the threat of nuclear destruction

934. The proposed land invasion of Japan was to be called Operation Downfall. However, once the decision was made to use nuclear bombs, the plan was never executed

935. The Japanese surrender was announced by Emperor Hirohito on 15 August 1945

936. The formal Japanese surrender was not signed until 2nd September (VJ Day - Victory over Japan)

937. The site chosen for the unconditional surrender of Japan was the *USS Missouri* - the flagship of the 3rd Fleet

938. Documents have revealed that if a third atomic bomb were needed, Tokyo would have been the target city

Bravery

939. The Victoria Cross – Britain's highest award for valour - was awarded 182 times to 181 recipients for action in the Second World War

940. 86 Victoria Cross awards were posthumous

941. Captain Charles Hazlitt Upham, VC & Bar served with the New Zealand 2nd Division and was the only person to be awarded the Victoria Cross (VC) twice during the Second World War. First in Crete in May 1941, and again at Ruweisat Ridge, during the Battle of El Alamein, in July 1942

942. The only Victoria Cross awarded on D-Day went to CSM Stanley Hollis of the Green Howards

943. The George Cross is the UK's second highest award, given for 'acts of the greatest heroism or for the most conspicuous courage in circumstances of extreme danger not in the direct presence of the enemy'

944. 143 George Crosses were awarded during the Second World War. 15 recipients were awarded the Bar to the George Cross for a second award

945. On 15 April 1942 King George VI conferred the George Cross onto the island of Malta; 'To honour her brave people I award the George Cross to the island fortress of Malta to bear witness to a heroism and devotion that will long be famous'

946. Created by Maria Dickin, the founder of the People's Dispensary for Sick Animals (PDSA) to honour the work of animals in the war, the Dickin Medal was a bronze medallion bearing the words 'For Gallantry' and 'We Also Serve'

947. The Dickin Medal was awarded to any animal that displayed conspicuous gallantry or devotion to duty while serving with any branch of the British Armed Forces or Civil Defence Units – it is commonly known as the Animal Victoria Cross

948. The first recipients of the award, in December 1943, were 3 pigeons serving with the Royal Air Force. White Vision, Winkie and Tyke all flew some 60 plus miles in bad weather to deliver messages that led to the rescue of a ditched aircrew in October 1943

949. The medal was awarded 54 times between 1943 and 1949, to 32 pigeons, 18 dogs, 3 horses and a cat, to acknowledge actions of gallantry or devotion during the Second World War

950. At the outbreak of war, the highest military award available in Germany was the Knights Cross of the Iron Cross

951. Throughout the course of the war, additional grades of the Knight's Cross were instituted. The Knights Cross with Oak Leaves was instituted in on 3 June 1940; Swords were added in July 1941; Diamonds were also added in same month and finally Golden oakleaves were introduced in December 1944

952. In total, 7.313 Knights Crosses were awarded. 883 Knights Cross winners also received Oakleaves, and 160 were awarded the Oak Leaves with Swords. Only 27 people received the Oak Leaves with Swords and Diamonds

953. The last Knights Cross to be awarded was given to Naval officer Wolfgang Feller who won the award on 17 June 1945 - more than a month after VE Day - for his role in helping clear the Baltic Sea of mines

954. The only person to receive the Grand Cross of the Iron Cross was Hermann Göring who was awarded the unique decoration on 19 July 1940 for his command of the *Luftwaffe* during the defeat of France

955. The original Grand Cross of the Iron Cross Göring received from Hitler was destroyed in an air-raid, but he had extras made including a special one made from platinum. He was wearing the platinum cross when he was captured in 1945

956. It is estimated that around 4,500,000 Iron Cross 2nd Class awards were distributed during the war

957. There were 29 female recipients of the Iron Cross 2nd Class, with 2 also winning the 1st Class award

958. 43 Knights Cross awards were bestowed on individuals serving with German allies including Japanese Fleet Admiral Isoruko Yamamoto

959. To receive the Iron Cross 1st Class, men needed to perform 3 or 4 further acts of bravery and courage on top of the one that earned them the Iron Cross 2nd Class

960. Between 300,000 and 575,000 Iron Cross 1st Class awards were given out during the war

961. Both Spain and Japan manufactured the Iron Cross. Japan did so for German sailors stationed in Tokyo

962. Unlike the Knights Cross of the Iron Cross where the ultimate decision of bestowal rested with Hitler, the authority to award either class of the Iron Cross was handed down to the divisional commanders who would send proposal lists to the Personnel Office of the Supreme Command of the Army for approval

963. The entire crew of U-29 were awarded the Iron Cross Second Class on 18 September 1939 in recognition of them sinking the British aircraft carrier HMS Courageous the previous day

964. The Spanish double-agent Juan Pujol Garcia (known as Arabel to the Germans and as Garbo to the British) was awarded the Iron Cross Second Class and the MBE

965. Only 6 sets of Golden Oak Leaves were manufactured, each consisting of an A-piece, made of 18 Carat gold with 58 real diamonds and a B-piece, made of 14 Carat gold with 68 real sapphires

966. Only 1 person was awarded the Golden Oak Leaves - Oberst (Colonel) Hans-Ulrich Rudel - who was a ground-attack pilot serving almost exclusively on the Eastern Front

967. Shot down over 24 times, Hans Rudel is credited with destroying over 500 tanks, 2,000 ground targets, the Russian battleship Marat, 2 cruisers and a destroyer, and was so successful against Russian forces that Joseph Stalin put up a 100,000 rouble ransom on his head

968. There were 473 Medal of Honor recipients during the war. One of which was the Unknown Soldier who rests at Arlington Cemetery

969. Only 7 African Americans were awarded the Medal of Honor for their actions in the war, but they had to wait until January 1997 to receive their awards

970. Private First Class Sadao Munemori was the only Japanese-American recipient of the Medal of Honor during the war

971. Since the end of the war, over 2-dozen Medals of Honor have been awarded to men who were denied the Medal during the war due to their race, ethnicity, or religion

972. The latest Medal of Honor awarded for action in World War II was to US Army First Lieutenant Garlin Conner, whose Distinguished Service Cross was upgraded to the Medal of Honor in 2018. His widow, Pauline Conner, accepted the Medal on his behalf from President Donald Trump

973. Ranking just below the Medal of Honor was The Distinguished Service Cross and was awarded for extreme gallantry and risk of life in combat with the enemy. Just over 5,000 were awarded during the Second World War

974. 2 women – French Resistance Operative Jeannette Guyot and Virginia Hall who worked with British SOE and American OSS groups – were awarded the US Distinguished Service Cross

975. Maurice Britt was playing NFL for the Detroit Lions in 1941 before being called up for military service. Before his honourable discharge in December 1944, he had become the first soldier to be awarded the top 4 combat decorations the US had to offer: The Medal of Honor, The Distinguished Service Cross, The Silver Star and The Bronze Star with Valor device. He also won The Purple Heart with 3 Oakleaves, the US Army Commendation Medal, the Military Cross (UK) and the Medal of Military Valour (Italy)

976. During the war 12 soldiers, 3 airmen and 2 sailors received both the Medal of Honor and the Distinguished Service Cross

977. Up until 22 September 1943 the Purple Heart was awarded to US military personnel for both wounds received in action against the enemy or for meritorious performance of duty. After 22 September, the Legion of Merit was introduced by Congress and the practice of awarding the Purple Heart for meritorious service was discontinued

978. Japan's highest military order during the war was the Order of the Golden Kite – awarded for bravery or leadership in command or battle

979. The order consisted of 7 classes. Enlisted rank soldiers were eligible for the 7th–5th classes, non-commissioned officers were eligible for the 6th–4th classes, junior officers for the 5th–3rd classes, field grade officers for the 4th–2nd classes and general officers for the 3rd-1st classes

980. During the Pacific War with the USA, 630,000 Orders of the Golden Kite were awarded across all grades

981. The Légion d'honneur is the highest French order of merit. Established by Napoleon in 1802 it consisted of 5 levels, starting with Chevalier (Knight) and moving up to Officier (Officer) Commandeur (Commander) Grand Officier (Grand Officer) and Grand-Croix (Grand Cross)

Casualties

982. On 9 December 1939, 4031789 Corporal Thomas William Priday of the 1st Battalion, King's Shropshire Light Infantry became the first battle casualty of the British Army during WW2 when he was killed whilst on patrol in Luttange, a small French town east of Metz on the Franco/German border.

983. It is impossible to give exact numbers, but reasonable estimates suggest that between 65,000,000 - 85,000,000 people were killed throughout the conflict. This number includes civilians and those killed by disease, illness and starvation as a result of the war. These numbers represent approximately 3% of the total 1940's population

984. There were between 20,000,000 -25,000,000 military deaths, including around 5 million soldiers who died while being held prisoner

985. Estimates suggest there were 25,000,000 men wounded in battle

986. Around 66% of all Second World War casualties were civilian - compared to just 5% in the First World War

987. 26,000,000 Soviet civilians perished in the war

988. Approximately 1,500,000 civilians were killed from aerial bombing throughout the conflict

989. The Soviet Union topped the table for military deaths with estimates ranging from 8,600,000 to 11,400,000 dead

990. Behind the Soviet Union, Germany suffered the second highest number of military deaths with estimates ranging between 4,400,000 and 5,000,000

991. Estimates suggest around 180,000 *Waffen-SS* soldiers were killed in action, with 70,000 listed as missing and 400,000 wounded

992. The Soviet Red Army claim to be responsible for 76% of all German war casualties

993. Great Britain suffered 383,700 military deaths along with almost as many again wounded

994. The British civilian death toll was around 70,000 – largely due to enemy bombing raids. In the First World War, just 2,000 civilians were killed

995. The USA lost 407,300 military personnel dead with another 671,801 wounded

996. Yugoslavia suffered more military casualties than both the United Kingdom and the USA with around 446,000 deaths

997. The number of Chinese killed by Japan during WW2 was more than the number of Jews killed in the Holocaust

998. Accounts vary, but although Poland suffered a relatively low 240,000 military deaths, there were between 5,000,000 and 6,000,000 Polish civilians killed during The Holocaust and various other crimes against humanity

999. The largest Second World War American military cemetery in Europe is the Lorraine American Cemetery. Situated just outside the French town of St. Avold it contains 10,489 American war dead

1000. The largest German military cemetery in the world is Ysselsteyn in The Netherlands – it contains 31,598 German war dead from both world wars

1001. The Bayeux War Cemetery is the largest Second World War cemetery of Commonwealth soldiers in France. Located in Bayeux, Normandy, it holds 4,144 Commonwealth burials, 338 of which are unidentified. There are also over 500 war graves of men from other nationalities, mostly German

References

All Hell Let Loose: The World at War 1939-1945 by Sir Max Hastings (Harper Press, 2012)
Arnhem: The Complete Story of Operation Market Garden 17-25 September 1944 by William Buckingham (Amberley Publishing, 2019)
Barbarossa. The Russian-German Conflict 1941-45 by Alan Clark (W&N, 2001)
The Battle of Britain by James Holland (Corgi, 2011)
The Battle of Midway by Craig L. Symonds (Oxford University Press, 2013)
Berlin: The Downfall 1945 by Anthony Beevor (Penguin, 2007)
The Blitz: The British Under Attack by Juliet Gardiner (Harper Press, 2011)
Blitzkrieg: Myth, Reality and Hitler's Lightning War - France, 1940 by Lloyd Clark (Atlantic Books, 2016)
Bomber Command by Sir Max Hastings (Pan Military Classics, 2012)
The British Home Front 1939-45 by Martin Brayley (Osprey, 2005)
Burma '44 by James Holland (Corgi, 2017)
The D-Day Encyclopaedia by Barrett Tillman (Regnery History, 2014)
D-Day: Minute by Minute by Johnathon Mayo (Short Books Ltd, 2015)
Day of Infamy by Walter Lord (Owl Books, 2001)
The Desert War by Alan Moorehead (Aurum Press Ltd, 2017)
Finest Hour by Tim Clayton & Phil Craig (Hodder & Stoughton, 1999)
The Illustrated Encyclopaedia of Weapons of World War II by Chris Bishop (Amber, 2016)
Invasion! D-Day and Operation Overlord in 100 Moments by Scott Addington (Unicorn Press, 2019)
Kursk. The Greatest Battle by Lloyd Clark (Headline Review, 2012)
The Miracle of Dunkirk: The True Story of Operation Dynamo by Walter Lord (Open Road Media 2017)
Okinawa 1945 by George Feifer (Tempus, 2005)
The Pacific War 1941-45 by John Costello (William Morrow, 1982)
Reaching for the Sky – The RAF in 100 Moments by Scott Addington (Unicorn Press, 2018)

The Second World War by Anthony Beevor (Weidenfeld & Nicolson, 2012)

Snow and Steel: Battle of the Bulge 1944-45 by Peter Caddick-Adams (Arrow, 2015)

Spitfire. History of a Legend by Mike Lepine (Sona Books, 2020)

The SS – A New History by Adrian Weale (Abacus, 2012)

Stalingrad by Anthony Beevor (Penguin, 2007)

Operation Valkyrie: The German Generals' Plot Against Hitler by Pierre Galante (Cooper Square Press, 2002)

The War in the West Vol 1 – Germany Ascendant by James Holland (Corgi 2016)

World War II at Sea: A Global History by Craig L Symonds (OUP USA, 2018)

World War 2 – The Definitive Visual Guide by DK & Richard Holmes (DK, 2015)

Wings by Patrick Bishop (Atlantic Books, 2012)

WW2: A Layman's Guide by Scott Addington (CreateSpace, 2016)

I really hope you enjoyed this fact book. If you did enjoy it, please consider leaving a positive review on Amazon or wherever you purchased this book from. Positive reviews help this book become more discoverable for other people looking for Second World War facts!

Don't forget, if you want even more facts, head on over to www.scottaddington.com and pick up a free e-book:
500 Fantastic First World War Facts

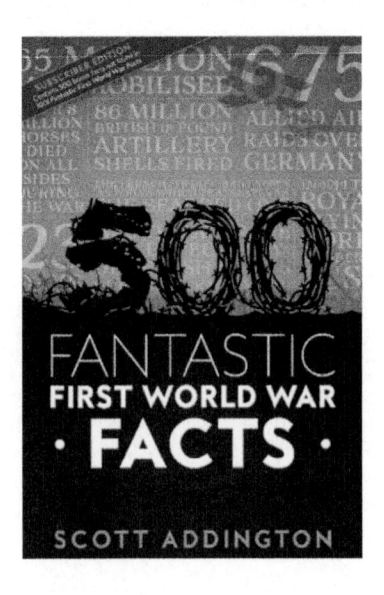

1001 Sensational Second World War Facts

1001 Sensational Second World War Facts

Printed in Great Britain
by Amazon